Philadelphia Plus One
A Traveler's Guide

Philadelphia Plus One
A Traveler's Guide

Nancy Sokoloff

Illustrated by
Susan DeCurtis

WhyNot Press
Philadelphia, Pennsylvania

Cover design by Susan DeCurtis
Book design by Susan DeCurtis and Del Kahn

Copyright © 1987
All Rights Reserved
WhyNot Press
314 South Third St.
Philadelphia, Pennsylvania 19106

Printed by R. R. Donnelley and Sons Company.

This book is dedicated to all travelers and to my husband, the man at the wheel, in particular.

Other Days, Other Ways

"I must, without vanity, say that I have led the greatest colony into America that ever a man did upon a private credit, and the most prosperous beginnings that ever were in it are to be found amoung us."

Arms of Wm. Penn, Proprietor of Pennsylvania.

Contents

* indicates full coverage in book text

Annapolis 21
Antiquing 25
    Notices in specialized magazines
    The Philadelphia Inquirer antique columns
    Auction pages of local and Philadelphia papers
    Adamsville
    Lancaster
    Mullica Hill
    Moorestown
    Haddonfield
    New Castle
    Eastern Shore towns
    *Cape May
    *Atlantic City
    *New Hope
Atlantic City 29
    Race course
    Gardiner's Basin
    Fischer greenhouses
    Brigantine Wildlife Refuge
    Somers Mansion
    "Old Abe"
    Cape May-Lewes Ferry
Avondale, Home of a Patriot 33
Baltimore 37
    Johns Hopkins University
    Baltimore Museum of Art
    Trade Center
    HarborPlace
    McCormick Spice House
    Maryland Science Center
    Peabody Institute

Stafford Hotel
Enoch Pratt Free Library
Basilica of the Assumption
Walters Art Gallery
Fire museum
Streetcar museum
Ft. McHenry
Baltimore Zoo
Cylburn Arboretum

The Barnes Foundation 41
Bartram's Gardens 45
Batsto 49
Biking 53
    Greater Philadelphia Biking Coalition
    Valley Forge National Historical Park
    Wissahickon Free Wheelers
    *Longwood Gardens
    Cape May Park
    *Cape May
    *New Castle
    Chestertown
    *Amish Country

Brandywine Valley 57
    West Chester County Historical Society
    *The Main Line
    *Waynesborough
    Chadds Ford
    Brandywine River Museum
    "Mushroom Capital"
    Brandywine Battlefield
    Barnes-Brinton House
    *Longwood Gardens
    *Winterthur
    Nemours
    Delaware Art Museum
    *Delaware Museum of Natural History

Bryn Athyn 63
    Glencairn
    Bryn Athyn Cathedral

Buten Museum 67

Contents 11

Canoeing 71
    Delaware River
    Shawnee-on-the-Delaware
    Dingman's Ferry
    *Pocono Mountains
    Lum's Pond
    Chester River Trail
    Batsto River
    *Pine Barrens

Cape May 77

Caves and Caverns 81
    Indian Echo Caverns
    Crystal Cave
    Lost River Cavern
    Center Hall

Chestnut Hill 85

Coal Mine Adventure 89

A Day in the Amish Country 93
    Lancaster Pike
    Amish Information Center
    Strasburg
    Columbia
    Lancaster
    York

Delaware Museum of Natural History 99

Dolls, Dolls, Dolls! 103
    Mary Merritt Museum
    Nostalgia House
    Lemay's doll hospital
    Doll shows, auctions, sales, galleries
    Brandywine River Museum (Christmas exhibit)

The Eastern Shore 107
    St. Michael's
    Easton
    Oxford
    Trappe

Englishtown Auction and Flea Market 113

Ephrata Cloister 115

Fliers All! 119
    Willow Grove Naval Air Station
    Wilmington Airport
    Lumberton
    Wings Airfield
    Dutch Hot Air Balloon Championship
    Sweet Sky
    Chatsworth
    Millville Airport
    Valley Forge Signal Seekers
The Franklin Mint Museum 123
Freedoms Foundation 127
Gettysburg 131
The Great Outdoors 135
    Estate gardens (Longwood, Winterthur, Nemours, Barnes)
    Arboretums
    Nature conservancies
    Watershed associations
    Nature centers
    Wildlife preserves and centers
    Nature preserves
Green Hills Farm 141
Hagley Museum and Mills 145
Harpers Ferry 149
Historic Fallsington 153
Hope Lodge 157
Hopewell Village 161
Horses 165
    Military parades
    Grand Prix
    Devon Horse Show
    Radnor Hunt
    Dressage
    Point-to-Point
    Gold Cup Grand Prix
    Appaloosa Show
    Trail riding competitions
    Pleasure riding
    Horse breeding (Arabians, racing, etc.)

A Journey on the Great Germantown Road 171
    Germantown historic complex (six sites)
    Germantown Museum
    Howell House
    Bechtel House
    Clark-Watson House
    Cliveden
    Upsala
    Germantown Mennonite Information Center
    Concord Schoolhouse
    Loudon
    Stenton
    Grumblethorpe
    Ebenezer Maxwell House
Longwood Gardens 181
The Main Line 185
    Overbrook
    Merion
    Narberth
    Wynnewood
    Ardmore
    Haverford
    Bryn Mawr
    Rosemont
    Villanova
    St. David's
    Wayne-Strafford
    Berwyn
    Paoli
    Malvern-Exton and beyond
The Mercer Mile 191
Mill Grove 195
Morven 199
New Castle 203
Pennsbury Manor 207
Peter Wentz Farmstead 211
The Pine Barrens 215
The Poconos 219
Pottsgrove 223
The Pusey Plantation 227

Railroading 231
    Pine Creek Railroad
    East Broad Top
    Strasburg Railroad
    Gettysburg Railroad
    Railroad Museum of Pennsylvania
    *Thomas Newcomen Museum
    Toy Train Museum
    Traintown, U.S.A.
    Paoli Local

Renault Winery 237

A Ride on the New Hope Canal 241

Stargazing 245
    Villanova University
    Princeton University
    University of Delaware
    Haverford College
    Swarthmore College
    New Jersey State Museum
    Willingboro
    Astronomical societies

Steamtown, U.S.A. 249

Thomas Newcomen Library and Museum 253

Tubing 257
    Brandywine areas
    Shawnee-on-Delaware
    Point Pleasant

Valley Forge 261

Valley Forge Military Academy 265

Washington Crossing 269

Waynesborough 271

The Wharton Esherick Museum 277

Wheatland 281

Wheaton Village 285

Winterthur 289

Wright's Ferry Mansion 293

Yellow Springs 297

York 301

Illustrations

Little Girl with Flowers (Acknowledgments)
Chase Lloyd House (Annapolis)
Antiques (Antiquing)
Boardwalk at Night (Atlantic City)
Gates at Avondale (Avondale, Home of a Patriot)
Inner Harbor (Baltimore)
A Garden Scene (Bartram's Gardens)
Bicycle (Biking)
Farmhouse (Brandywine Valley)
Glencairn Museum (Bryn Athyn)
Wedgwood Plate (Buten Museum)
Canoe (Canoeing)
Victorian Windows (Cape May)
Cave (Caves and Caverns)
Coal Miner (Coal Mine Adventure)
Amish Country (A Day in the Amish Country)
Bear and Friends (Delaware Museum of Natural History)
Dolls, Dolls, Dolls! (Dolls, Dolls, Dolls!)
Loon Decoy (The Eastern Shore)
Private Plane (Fliers All!)
Soldier at Gettysburg (Gettysburg)
Heron in the Great Outdoors (The Great Outdoors)
Chinese People (Green Hills Farm)
Wheel at Hagley Museum (Hagley Museum and Mills)
Window in Hopewell Village (Hopewell Village)
Horse and Rider (Horses)
American Antiques at Mercer Museum (The Mercer Mile)
Front Door in New Castle (New Castle)
Beehive at Pennsbury Manor (Pennsbury Manor)
Pine Barrens (Pine Barrens)
Window at Pottsgrove (Pottsgrove)
Railroading (Railroading)
Stargazing (Stargazing)

Washington at Valley Forge (Valley Forge)
Glassware at Wheaton (Wheaton Village)
Wharton Esherick Studio (Wharton Esherick Museum)
Queen Anne Chair (Winterthur)
Gazebo at Yellow Springs (Yellow Springs)

How to Get There from Here

With this book you can preplan a vacation in a wide region of the Mid-Atlantic states of Pennsylvania, New Jersey, Delaware, and Maryland. There are also chapters on special interests such as historic houses, ethnic lifestyles, trains, antiques, or horses!

Philadelphia with four centuries of history has easy one-day-and-return distances to a multitude of fascinating sites. To the north are the relatively unspoiled Pocono Mountains featuring woods, lakes, and some resort hotels. The Lancaster Valley "Dutch country" lies to the west where Amish and Mennonite citizens are happy to include you in a very different way of life. To the south is the great Chesapeake Bay, its eastern shore edged with lovely old towns with yet another lifestyle, and to the east are New Jersey and the "Shore" with miles of Atlantic Ocean and barrier islands.

Sites have direct routing starting from the "Wedding Cake," Philadelphia's City Hall, in the center of the city. All sites have phone numbers and background material so you may have a better appreciation of what you will see. Not included are commercial outlets, theme parks, hotels, or restaurants. New York and Washington are a comfortable day's journey away. Use a good area map with the text for best results.

The *Philadelphia Inquirer* newspaper carries an extensive weekend calendar, many feature event stories, and good columns for specialized interests.

Visitors are welcome at all the sites, and although English is spoken at all the locations, you may hear local phrases such as, "Use the pike," or, "Go by the old river road." Just be sure to use your maps and ask for exact routes or street names.

William Penn wearing his broadbrim stands atop City Hall with outstretched hand to welcome you. We all hope you come back again and soon!

Acknowledgments

Just as the subject matter of this book is a whole comprised of many parts so is the fine art of production of the volume in your hand. It could not have been done alone. Special thanks must go first to my husband who suffered and enjoyed visiting all these sites with me on fair days and foul. Thanks to my publisher and his immediate grasp of the "WhyNot Press". Special thanks to the patient and careful lady who produced the typescript with its needed corrections and to the representative of our printing company who led us through the maze of getting the book in shape to present to you. The illustrations speak well for themselves.

And to Warner, Pace, Stephanie, Ryan and Matthew who may wonder what all the fuss was about but whom we hope will use the book and learn to know their surrounding countryside.

Nancy Sokoloff
1986

Annapolis

This old town on the Chesapeake Bay was a flourishing port in the 1700s when Baltimore was still a growing village. Because of its attractive, compact size you will find good walking in the historic part of town and wharfside. There are tour services available but much to see on your own in this bayside gem which has retained its charm thanks to its citizens' continuing vigilance.

The old Mark House at the city dock has been restored and is indeed a busy marketplace today. Built in 1858, it is still selling wonderful Chesapeake Bay seafood, the local specialty delight.

The Old Victualling Warehouse and Customs and Mark House once served as general meeting places where one could buy and sell wares, sign aboard a ship, or sell farm-grown wares to outgoing ships. It has a good triorama of the early days of Annapolis, when its waterfront was one of the busiest on the Colonial seacoast.

In its naturally guarded location the town proved a challenge to the British who tried attacking, blockading, and infiltrating it at various times without much success. The town was formerly named Providence, but when designated the capital of Maryland, it changed its name in honor of the English Queen Anne. It was also then raised to the rank of a city with forty houses, a free school, and a brick church! Many of its citizens, like much of Maryland, were ardent Loyalists and unsympathetic to the Colonial cause of Revolution. A great proportion were devout Roman Catholics but discarded religious and political differences when George Washington came to the old Senate Chamber to resign his commission as General of the Continental Army.

Annapolis was the capital of the United States between November 26, 1783, and August, 1784, and it was in these same chambers that the Treaty of Paris was finally ratified, ending the Revolutionary War.

There is a short visual presentation, and you can take a twenty-minute guided tour of the 1772 building daily except on Thanksgiving, Christmas, and New Year's Day. There is no admission fee. The Visitors Center is also conveniently located, so you can select information of interest to you.

There are beautiful, restored houses running the length of two blocks with four of the finest Colonial homes to be seen in America. Everyone admires the Hammond-Harwood House with its graceful doorway at 19 Maryland Avenue. In the Chase-Lloyd House across the street Mary Taylor Lloyd, the governor's daughter, married Francis Scott Key. The William Pace House, which has had a checkered ownership career, is now restored after careful archeological excavations that revealed much original stonework. The great formal gardens must not be missed! It has a trellis bridge, a domed pavilion, and a fish-shaped pond that once held the "golden carp" that were a colonial rarity. At Christmastime many special tours of the houses decorated in period cheer are available. For specifics about these call the Ann Arundel Tourism Office at (301)268-TOUR.

Everyone wants to visit the United States Naval Academy on the banks of the Severn River where it joins the great Bay. Located on King George Street, the Academy can be seen on a walking tour leaving from Ricketts Hall. The grounds are open to the public Monday through Saturday from 9:00 a.m. to 5:00 p.m., and on Sunday from 12:00 noon to 5:00 p.m. There is, of course, no charge, but the tours do require a fee. The chapel is the most outstanding feature of the campus; it contains the body of John Paul Jones, famous high-spirited naval officer we all know from history books. The Naval Museum has ship models, uniforms with all sorts of swords to go with them, and other memorabilia.

Other parts of the town have good shops, galleries, and the old Middleton Tavern, also restored, which is located at 2 Market Square.

There are many harbor cruises and one at 10:00 a.m. that will take you to St. Michael's on the Bay for the whole day.

The town today maintains its excellence as a shipbuilding and designing center for sailing yachts. Regattas on the Bay are popular with the entire region, and the large power and sailboat show in October draws crowds from the whole country.

Routing: Take I-95 south to Route 896 and continue south on Route 896 to U.S. 40. Cross U.S. 40 to Route 301. Go south on Route 301 and watch for Annapolis signs.

Annapolis 23

Notes

Antiquing

Some of the finest antiquing in the U.S.A. is found in eastern Pennsylvania, New Jersey, Delaware, and Maryland. Someone has been heard to say, "You are in the heart of heavendom!" Depending on your particular field of interest, you will find wide diversity throughout every season of the year.

There are large, internationally patronized shows in Philadelphia, New York, Baltimore, and Washington with elegant treasures for sale. Top dealers only are asked to exhibit, and many save their finest wares for these beautifully produced events. Most have additional lectures, luncheon-meet-the-dealer days by reservation. Most are programmed for the spring months of April and May, so consult the good antique magazines, the local press, and the local Visitors Bureau for dates.

Many shows are annual benefits for a local charity or institution, so if the Philadelphia Visitors Bureau does not have dates, ask the name of the cause and seek out a chairman (usually in the locale). Their planning committees will be very glad to send you printed advance materials.

Throughout the weekends year round indoor and outdoor shows that represent high-quality furniture, rugs, china, glass, quilts, paintings, books, toys, tinwares, and period clothing abound. Almost all also offer delicious regional food specialties. (You certainly do not have to settle for tepid hot dogs!) Special brochures for the eastern Pennsylvania counties can be had by calling their County Tourist Bureaus. The Philadelphia Visitors Center can supply these numbers. Call (215)636-3300 or (215)568-6599.

Scan *The Philadelphia Inquirer's* antique page and the excellent weekend column by their top authority, Lita Solis-Cohen, one of the best in the nation.

There are also hundreds of good antique galleries and shops open every day throughout the countryside in all four states for browsing and buying. Some specialize (dolls, furnishing, books, etc.); others have items of one broad period. All the proprietors seem to enjoy discussing antiques with either new or seasoned collectors.

There are always scheduled auctions, but these are quite a different thing! Prices are not listed, and you are on your own on bidding. At auctions there are usually professional dealers well acquainted with the offerings and also seeking to buy. Frequently, several will form a consortium to purchase an article or a lot of great value. Institutions, such as historical houses or museums, often use these pools to buy for them in a knowledgeable way, so that many things are returned to original sites. This can drive the prices up, so keep alert!

Estate auctions are popular and have older items that may exactly suit your own taste and purse, so go and have fun. These are listed in the local papers with ads. There is also usually a special column listing them.

There are also regular weekly sales held in rural areas such as Adamsville near Reading and Lancaster, Pennsylvania. Often brochures can be obtained from nearby Information Centers. It is also well worth crossing the Delaware River to New Jersey, which has good shops in Mullica Hill. Moorestown and Haddonfield also offer annual and seasonal sales. Trenton follows this style too. To the south the Chesapeake and Tidewater areas tend to present lovely, more elegant furnishings suitable for homes more formal than the Pennsylvania country styles.

Cape May and Atlantic City both have many dealers, and visits to their big annual sales will also give you a stroll on the boardwalk and good food.

Antiquing is educational, good fun, satisfying, tantalizing, often profitable, and generally a purse-eater. It is also practically incurable!

Routing: Consult the Philadelphia Visitors Bureau, map in hand, for your preferred destination.

Notes

Atlantic City

"On the Boardwalk in Atlantic City" is a bit of nostalgia that can still be enjoyed by all the family today. The many casinos with glitzy entertainment and gambling have made a vast difference, of course, but there is still much to see, do, and enjoy in this old seaside town without stepping a foot inside casino doors.

The Atlantic Ocean still rolls on the sandy beach, and the famous saltwater taffy candy is available in wonderful, chewy flavors. There are bathers, sun fanciers, and bicyclers galore. The latter have been given "the run" of the famous boardwalk from 6:00 to 10:00 a.m. each day, and you can either join them or watch them with awe. There are little yellow tram cars that can take you to see the sights of the many shops, restaurants, and the passing parade at any time. Artists show their works in Gordon's Alley's popular shops, and there are lots of good places to eat at every price.

Within easy driving are the Atlantic City Race Course; Lucy the Elephant ("walk through and come out alive!") which has long been a popular landmark; a recreational seaside village in Gardiner's Basin; the Fischer Greenhouses, where more than 100,000 violets are on dazzling show, and, of course, the fall Miss America Pageant in Convention Hall. The Brigantine Wildlife Refuge, open from sunrise to sunset, is a must for bird-watchers studying migrations on the flyways. Its 20,000 acres of trails and auto tours are perfect for photography year round.

After the Civil War, families and friends brought trunks, servants, and sandpails for a month's or a summer's stay at the grand hotels or comfortable boardinghouses. The Somers Mansion, built in 1720 and furnished with authentic antiques, still survives and is open, free to the public, as the home of the County Historical Society in nearby Somers Point.

In 1857 the Absecon Lighthouse ("Old Abe") was first lighted to warn pleasure and commercial vessels from the offshore reefs. One hundred sixty-seven feet high, it is still a favorite landmark in a city park.

For sports lovers, there are golf, tennis, boxing, and racing. Marinas have all facilities for sailing or power boating. Fishing never loses its allure, and daily reports can be read in *The Philadelphia Inquirer* or heard on local stations.

You can combine the day with a trip to Batsto Village (New Jersey) or a two-hour ride on the Cape May-Lewes Ferry across Delaware Bay, where you will see large tankers waiting to be called in by the harbormaster for unloading or departures.

Daily updated information can be had from the Atlantic City Visitors Bureau ((609)345-7536). Rain or shine, the Jersey shore is still one of the best places to be!

Routing: Call the Atlantic City Visitors Bureau for specific routes to your preferred sites.

Notes

Avondale, Home of a Patriot

This fine county seat is one of the many historic houses outside of Philadelphia. Built by Thomas Lieper as a summer residence in a quiet, wooded setting by a wide stream, it is a good reminder of the isolation that made each plantation or smaller homestead self-sufficient in living.

Young Lieper arrived in the New World in 1763 as an orphaned immigrant from Scotland. He wasted no time in establishing himself as an energetic tobacco merchant and soon became a snuff manufacturer, which eventually repaid him with a large fortune.

Lieper was one of the first to advocate rupture with the British Crown and immediately put up 5,000 pounds to finance "The Cause." He and twenty-seven other impassioned citizens met in Carpenters' Hall in Philadelphia to organize the famous Light Horse of the city, which today is known as The First Troop. During the Revolution he accepted several posts. He provided escorts with the Light Horse for the large amounts of monies transferred by the new government, served in major battles at Brandywine, Germantown, Trenton, Princeton, and Monmouth, and with the financier Robert Morris became a second generous donor to funds for the Revolution.

When the war became more than impassioned speeches, Lieper realized that no one around Philadelphia knew how to produce saltpeter or niter mixed with sulphate to make gunpowder. While committees experimented for months with poor results, Lieper converted his snuff mills on Crum Creek to gunpowder factories. Eight factories were certified by the Committee of Safety of the First Continental Congress for the conversion to powder mills and bullet factories. Five of these eight belonged to industrious Lieper.

Following the end of the war, the Patriotic Association agreed to mutual support and Lieper's signature followed Thomas Paine's.

Philadelphia, a hotbed of opinions, became the national capital, and Lieper, along with Jefferson, became one of the founders of the Republican party (now the Democratic party).

His acres of quarries on Crum Creek flourished, and he built lovely Strathaven Hall, now known as Avondale, where for many years distinguished visitors were received, including the first nine Presidents of the United States. Its unique front gate, its handsome approach, and beautiful interior are a rewarding experience to see. Five of the original seven buildings remain from the original plantation village.

Lieper, always a concerned citizen, also contributed funds to new canals and post roads. His own Lieper Canal was used from 1829 to 1852, when railroads took over. This enterprising and devoted American is not much noted in our history books but remained a steadfast and helpful citizen all his life.

The house and grounds of Avondale are open for a small charge, Saturday and Sunday from 1:00 to 4:00 p.m. except January, February, and March. There are often special celebrations and decorations you will enjoy, so call first ((215)566-6365). Among other pleasures there is lovely picnicking by the stream. You are not far from historic Waynesborough and old Saint David's Church outside Wayne, so you can make a country day of it.

Routing: Take the Schuylkill Expressway west to City Line Avenue (Route 1). Go south on Route 1. Turn right onto Route 252 and follow to Rose Valley Road. Turn left and go to Avondale Road. Turn right.

Notes

Baltimore

This historic city has revitalized itself in many good restorations and new centers without losing its special Southern grace. A sheer delight to visit, it is both a large, busy port and a city of former styles and ambiance.

It is easily reached either directly or through more picturesque country roads of Chester County horse country with its farms, fieldstone houses, and handsome estates set by running streams. Use a good map for these routes.

This 200-year-old port on the Chesapeake Bay has seen the earliest explorers, Indians, divided loyalties in Colonial and Revolutionary days, Civil War participation, and has still retained its peace, gracious manners, and lovely style.

World-renowned Johns Hopkins University at 24th and Charles Street has its famed Medical School and sits adjacent to the large Baltimore Museum of Art on Museum Drive (open Tuesday through Saturday, 11:00 a.m. to 4:00 p.m., Sunday, 1:00 to 4:00 p.m.).

Center city is easy walking, and Charles Street makes a good backbone. From the twenty-seventh floor of the nearby World Trade Center you have a perfect view and panorama of the Harbor and surrounding countryside. Designed by I. M. Pei, it has good exhibits of city history.

Follow the redbrick pavement at its side to innovative Harbor Place with promenades, 125 shops and restaurants, the frigate *Constellation,* and the wonderful Aquarium with 8,000 specimens of aquatic life, a rain forest, and a shark ring!

On nearby Light Street you are invited into the Colonial rooms of the McCormick Spice Company to learn the romance of spices, coffees, and teas with delicious samples.

The Maryland Science Center is at the opposite end on West Shore and is full of "please touch" exhibits all the family can enjoy. Once fashionable Mt. Vernon Place lies between Cathedral and St. Paul's streets. It is still lined with mansions now well used for institutional purposes of the Walters Art Gallery and the Maryland Historical Society a few steps away. Here are fine period rooms, Baltimore paintings and silver, and a fine collection of ship models. The Walters Art Gallery is housed in a reproduction of a Genoa palazzo and has a vast holding of wide range given to the city by a father-son collecting family.

Across the street is the Peabody Institute, a conservatory of music donated by international banker George Peabody. Its library, open to the public, houses original scores by Beethoven, Handel, and Grieg. Around the corner on Washington Place is the Stafford Hotel, once the dueling grounds for impulsive gentlemen and also used by Baltimore society families as a residence during the "Season."

The whole area is dotted with shops, galleries, and restaurants and is a good meeting place if your group wants to pursue different interests.

Four-hundred Cathedral Street holds the enormous collection of the Enoch Pratt Free Library, one of the finest in the United States, and includes original works of Edgar Allen Poe, who scribbled in a garret nearby.

On Cathedral and Mulberry streets is the Basilica of the Assumption, the first Roman Catholic cathedral in the United States. On the second and fourth Sundays tours are given, but it is open at other times so you may see its beautiful interior.

Ask for the news sheet *The Baltimore Times* at a shop along the way. It has a good city map; a long list of attractions; historic houses; directions to the wonderful old Lexington Market, where food is presented by the acre for buying and eating; the fire museum; and the streetcar museum. It also notes the Baltimore Museum of Industry with its recreation of an old clothing factory, a machine shop, and a printing shop.

Fort McHenry, the starshaped fort in Baltimore Harbor, was the site of our victory over the British in 1812, and its flag inspired Francis Scott Key to write what is now our national anthem.

Also interesting to patriots is the Shot Tower at 801 Fayette Street. There is no admission to the sound and light show.

Seek out the zoo, the 200 acres of Druid Hill, or the 176 acres of Cylburn Arboretum at 4915 Greenspring Avenue. The Conservatory has enchanting year-round flowering displays from 10:00 a.m. to 4:00 p.m. daily.

There is more to see and do in Baltimore than one day can hold, but you will get a good feeling of our history to the south. If you decide to spend a weekend or several days, you are not far from Annapolis and the Eastern Shore full of charm and good things to eat! Both the Bay Bridge and the tunnel are adventures!

Routing: Take I-95 south and exit onto U.S. Route 40 and proceed south to the center of Baltimore. Here it is best to use a map of the city.

Notes

The Barnes Foundation

Anyone over fifty runs at the mere mention of the word Argyrol, that "awful brown stuff put in your nose to run disgustingly down your throat!" This cure-all for nasty childhood noses and colds was invented and patented by one Dr. Albert Barnes, who, with clever marketing, made fame and fortune with this silver-nitrate compound. Antibiotics were as yet undiscovered, and Argyrol became a mother's drugstore answer to prayer.

Barnes, son of a Philadelphia butcher, worked his way through Pennsylvania Medical School by boxing and semi-pro baseball. He dearly wished to become part of Philadelphia Society, but no doors opened to the man known to be both irritating and irritable in continuous battles. Barnes at last took his bride to the suburb of Merion Station and here began to indulge his obsession of art collecting.

The Barnes Impressionist paintings are one of the world's great collections, and they hang as he placed them row on row, floor to ceiling, in galleries he built for them. There are over a hundred Renoirs, important Cezannes, a Matisse mural, and an enormous Seurat. His taste in Old Masters leaves something to be desired, but a trip to "The Barnes" is a breathtaking experience!

Admission used to be strictly limited. No children were tolerated, and his staff worshiped the ground this tyrant walked on, referring to him in hushed tones as if today he might still come ranting in. Strict entry procedures prevail. Some of the public are admitted at the gatehouse, but prior reservations obtained by writing or calling ahead are preferred. Coats and pocketbooks must be deposited in a locker. There is no catalog. No brochures announce special exhibitions, for there are none. There are guards but no guides. There is no shop with colorful cards, art books, or reproductions. This is still very much a one-man show with its founder long dead.

The frustrated Dr. Barnes had a high belief in the common man and hung paintings in his factory where employees mixed, bottled, sealed, and packaged.

Because in his mind galleries should be opened only in a democratic way, he began his own series of art lectures, education courses, and books that are still very popular today. His factory workers were soon given additional jobs as preservationists or teachers under his firm hand. But his interest in the artist's approach to form, line, and color left much of the art world of the early 1900s far behind.

If Philadelphia did not respond, Europe did; for the paintings that shocked the Quaker City were well understood abroad. They knew Picasso, Modigliani, and Matisse very well! Soon directors of many distinguished museums asked to view his collection. Barnes's answer was invariably a terse "No!", a scathing comment, a broad joke, or unopened letters returned.

When Barnes was killed in a violent accident in 1951, publisher Walter Annenberg of Philadelphia filed suit to have the galleries opened and, after long pressure, a limited number of persons were admitted only on Fridays and Saturdays with the grudging statement that "they interrupted the school!" Today there are always people in the halls. The Barnes collection of paintings are breathtaking in spite of the crowded walls, so it is well to write or call ahead for reservations or take your chances that you may be admitted on the daily public quota.

Surrounding the building is a beautiful arboretum founded by his wife, who may have found her few tranquil hours there. This too is a showplace to be enjoyed.

This strange, unhappy man, far ahead of his time, brought art to every day workplaces much as offices are doing today, but he built his collection to surround himself with "his own kind of friends."

Philadelphia has several important museums and fine galleries in and out of the city, and this world-class museum is one not to be missed by those truly interested in fine art. The galleries and grounds are open by reservation. Call (215)667-0290.

Routing: Go west on the Schuylkill Expressway to City Line Avenue. Take City Line Avenue south and turn west onto Old Lancaster Road. Proceed on Old Lancaster Road to Latches Lane and go north to 300 Latches Lane. The Merion stop on the Paoli Local train takes you within walking distance. Call in advance for exact walking directions ((215)667-0290).

Notes

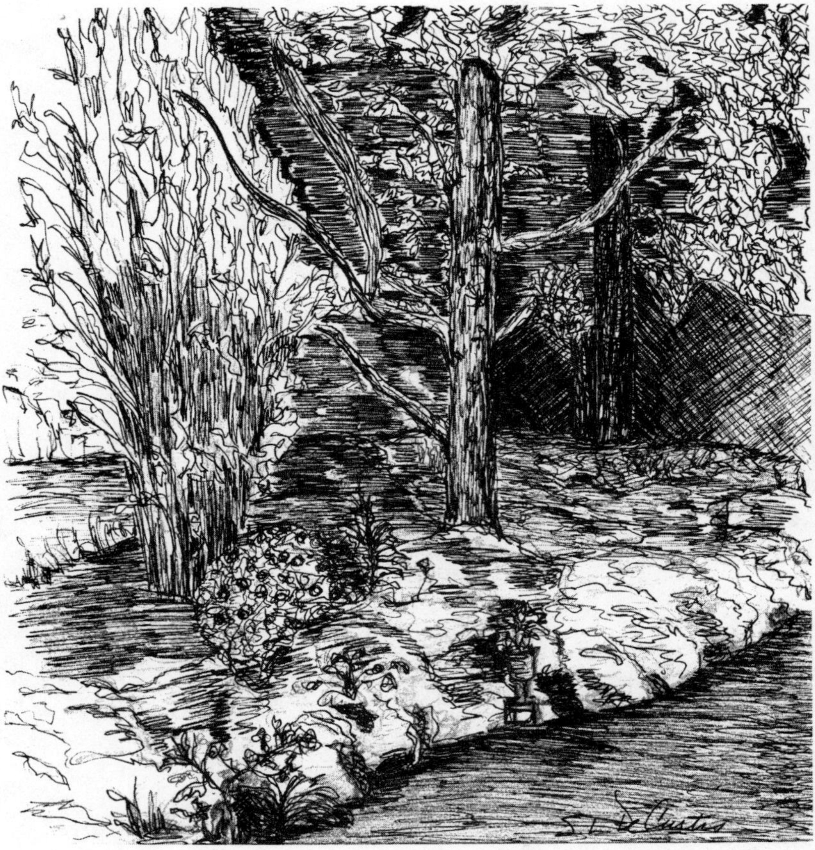

Bartram's Gardens

On the banks of the Schuylkill River at the west end of Philadelphia are the restored house and oldest botanical garden existing in America.

These twenty-seven acres belong to John Bartram, Royal Botanist to His Majesty King George III, and his son William, who followed in his distinguished horticultural footsteps.

Bartram was self-educated, poring over borrowed botanical books. After he learned Latin from books loaned to him by James Logan, Benjamin Franklin suggested he be retained by a prosperous London wool merchant as official Plant Collector. The two kept up a lively correspondence for thirty-five years, though Bartram never met his patron! Bartram's journeys took him from New York through the Deep South and as far West as the Ohio River, seeking seeds, roots, and plant speciments for propagation for overseas shipments. In an age where the natural sciences were most popular, Linnaeus praised him as "the greatest Natural Botanist in the world."

The Botanical Garden was begun by John Bartram "in the country aside from the busy city" in 1728. His son William later traveled throughout the colonies and into Spanish Florida country, selecting the best seeds and plants to grow and propagate. Strange new vegetables from here and abroad were planted with the curious shrubs and trees in the 300 acres of land considered by Bartram as his "garden." Here were The Yellow Wood with its trailing, southern wisteria-like flowers; the Toothache Tree, analgesic for sore gums; fragrant boxwood; and fig trees that endured the damp winters of this river valley. Even the hardy pomegranate rose annually against the warm farmhouse wall after dying down in unaccustomed frosts and snows.

In 1765 both Bartram and his son spent months in tropical Florida examining trees, vines, flowers, and shrubs unknown to the northern world. Later William traveled there alone for four years of exploration.

A skilled artist, his exquisite drawings illustrate his journal of the botanical world as he saw it with birds and animals included.

After his father's death, William continued the work and joined his brother in the farmhouse writing, drawing, gardening, and receiving and sending materials all over the world and to botanists Jefferson and Washington. The latter gentleman remarked that he found Bartram's country gardens "most disorderly in their natural state."

Philadelphian Andrew Eastwick eventually purchased the Bartram property with its cider mill, farms, orchards, and little springhouse. The City of Philadelphia was at last persuaded by his aging gardener that this treasure was within their bounds and needed special care. The sturdy farmhouse has a distinctive inset front entrance flanked by two wings and a dormered roof. It is today surrounded by seasonal delights of poppies, phlox, and lavender in a charming informal English style.

The garden and house are open daily Tuesday through Sunday from dawn to dusk for self-guided tours. Tours by reservation are from 10:00 a.m. to 4:00 p.m., Tuesday through Sunday from May to November (gardeners' weather!). Box lunches can be ordered in advance and a luscious tea is available at the trestle table. For information or reservations call (215)729-5281.

Canoeists can talk with the curator to arrange for a knowledgeable guide with whom to travel down the Schuylkill River to point out natural flora, fauna, and bird life of today.

Routing: Use a city map for directions to the garden and farmhouse at 54th and Lindbergh Boulevard or call (215)729-5281 for the clearest directions.

Notes

Batsto

The intriguing name Batsto (or baatsoo) used by the Scandinavian and Dutch settlers means "steam bath." It was also adopted by the New Jersey Lenape Indians to mean "bathing place," and many old deeds mention this as a favorite summering place for small tribes.

In 1766 Batsto Furnace was built on the shores of the Batsto River by Charles Read of Burlington, New Jersey, former ironmaster, lawyer, and Supreme Court Justice. But by the time of the Revolution the little valley had changed hands several times, though still supplying cannon and cannonballs for "The Cause." So important was this output that residents of the prosperous village were exempt from military service. Munitions for the War of 1812, water pipes for many East Coast cities, small iron products such as bolts, hinges, cartwheel rims, and the iron fence formerly surrounding Independence Square all were made at Batsto Furnace. In 1846 additional work came in the form of a glass factory supplying the large market for windowpanes, lamps, and lovely chandeliers. But by 1858 the remnants of the original Batsto Furnace were dismantled, and after ten more years the later glass industry was also gone.

After a ravaging fire the forlorn remains were purchased by Philadelphia financier Joseph Wharton, who developed the area into a farm for the raising of fine cattle, cranberries, and an experimental project in sugar beets. Lumbering accommodated a sawmill, and the small brickyard did a lively business. He also sought to promote the area as a summer resort with good roads, wagons for transport, open fields, and a shimmering lake. He sought interest in the area as a supply source for augmenting Philadelphia's short water supply from the streams and the deep aquifer of the Pine Barrens (see that text). After his death in 1909, the Wharton Tract of 100,000 acres was offered to the State of New Jersey for $1,000,000, but it was not until 1954 that they received the property.

Today you may wander at will around the thirty-five structures of the little village visiting its Victorian ironmaster's house on the hill, the old milk house and icehouse, stables, blacksmith and wheelwright shops, and the carriage house with its carts, carriages, and winter sleds. Cross the wooden bridge to the weaver's cottage next to his neighbor's potter's wheel. On some summer weekends you will see demonstrations of these arts. Through the village the Batsto River runs clear and golden brown, and around it are meadows with split rail fences to keep in grazing sheep. There are a good nature trail, birdwatching, and a lovely picnic area beside the lake. Bring your camera! There is also a good herb garden, authentically marked, that welcomes visitors. You are not far from many shore points such as Atlantic City or Wheaton Village.

Batsto Village is open Memorial Day through Labor Day from 10:00 a.m. to 6:00 p.m. and Labor Day to Memorial Day from 11:00 a.m. to 5:00 p.m. (admission).

Routing: Go north on Broad Street to Vine Street and turn right. Take Vine Street to the Benjamin Franklin Bridge. Take I-676 south to the Atlantic City Expressway and go east. Exit at Exit 28. Go north on Route 54 and turn right onto Route 542. Batsto is marked at the entrance.

Notes

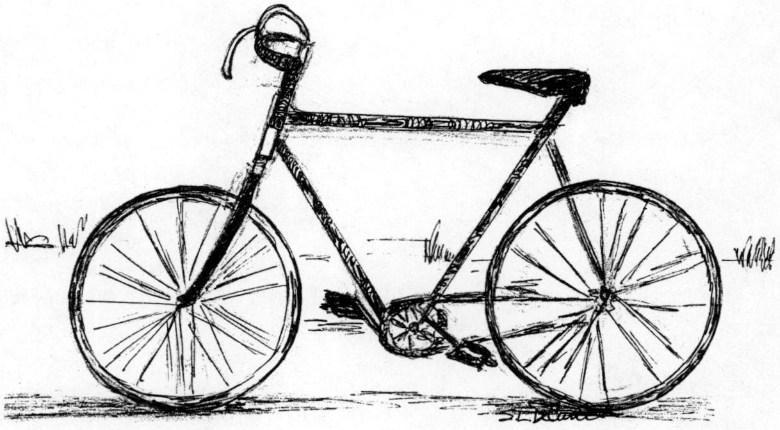

Biking

If you are a person whose spirit is freed on two wheels, the many areas around Philadelphia are for you!

The attractive rural countryside so close to this major city offers a wide variety of sights and sounds dear to the heart of the true biker. There are many organizations you can contact for vehicles, maps, routings, special group events, books, and sight-seeing trips that are a genuine pleasure. No less a person than Robert M. Scott, president of the Philadelphia Museum of Art, leads a bike ride in Fairmount Park and knows many back roads of Chester County. He has been known to arrive at formal dinner parties in black tie on his bike.

The Greater Philadelphia Bicycle Coalition has issued a good commuter map covering six counties in Pennsylvania, four in New Jersey, and one in Delaware. The map is on waterproof paper and is available at some bike shops and bookstores or through John Dowlin, Greater Philadelphia Bicycle Coalition, Box 8194, Philadelphia, Pennsylvania 19801.

Valley Forge National Historical Park has 6 miles of paved trail circling the park. Use caution, as it is also popular with joggers. Check in first at Park Headquarters for directions.

You can add mileage to your day if you call Wissahickon Free Wheelers, who stage weekly rides and welcome experienced bikers. Bring lunch and water. For information call (215)628-2786.

In summery weather there are fine rides in the evening through the blooms of Longwood Gardens in Kennett Square, Pennsylvania. Call to find dates and times (215)388-6741). Admission is requested.

The Delaware Valley Bike Club often sponsors good-length rides from Swarthmore College, Media, Pennsylvania. They are usually on Sunday, so call first to check ((215)352-3647).

There are quite a few bike races cropping up and bike-a-thons used for fund raising. The Philadelphia Visitors Bureau, located at 15th and JFK Boulevard, should have information on these ((215)568-6599). Also try calling the sports desk of *The Philadelphia Inquirer* ((215)854-2000).

If you are headed toward New Jersey, go to the trails in Cape May County Park. The Victorian town of Cape May is a gem in itself and perfect for biking while you admire the restored houses. It has a boardwalk, too, but check biking rules there first.

New Castle, Delaware, is another small town for a good, leisurely ride. It also has a lovely small park right on the Delaware River for picnics. Chestertown, Maryland, is also geared to slow sight-seeing. Stop at the White Swan Inn or a bookstore and ask for a walking tour map for a useful aid.

Long rides, short spins, leisurely look-sees, jaunts, or furious mileage pilers; there are acres to cover on wheels from Forbidden Drive in Chestnut Hill to a full day in the Amish Country. There you are enfolded in fertile fields; farms with horse-drawn plows; small, black buggy carriages; and stops for "wonderful good" regional foods.

Be sure that you know the safety rules and the appropriate gear and supplies. If you want, bring your own wheels and ride, ride, ride for one whole day right out of Philadelphia.

See contents and texts for the Amish Country, New Castle, Cape May, Chestnut Hill, Chestertown, and Valley Forge. Appropriate phone numbers are supplied there.

Routings: Check in at the Philadelphia Visitors Center for the best routes to your preferred sites. Keep your map handy.

Notes

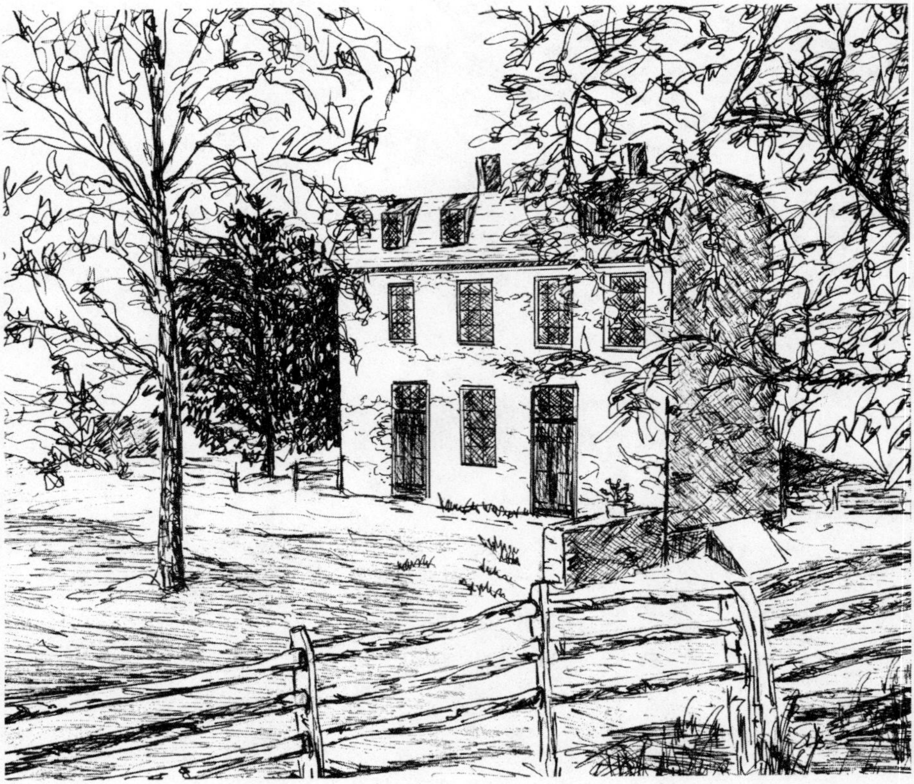

The Brandywine Valley

The Brandywine River rises in the hills of Pennsylvania and runs 60 miles to Wilmington, Delaware, on the banks of the busy, wide Delaware River. Miles of fertile farmlands are watered by this river. Once it gave power to more than 100 mills, was a route for shallow craft transporting people and wares to the south, and was the primary reason that young Du Pont in the 1700s located his gunpowder mills in this convenient area. Today historic towns, farms, restored inns, museums, college campuses, a battlefield, and busy ports exist along the banks of this brandy-colored stream. A pleasant change from the urban city of Philadelphia, the Brandywine Valley remains one of the prettiest on the East Coast.

There is a restored, old, square, stone tavern on Route 252 and Goshen Road that has lots of information for your particular tastes, for it is now headquarters for Delaware Visitors Center with good parking ((215)565-3679).

The Historical Society in the nearby town of West Chester, Pennsylvania, has excellent exhibits. Their Visitors Center is at 33 West Market Street ((215)431-6365). The old town is a small and pretty one, well cared for and carefully restored.

You will need one of its maps to travel the points we have mentioned below, and along the way you will discover signs for many more. It is impossible to do it all in one day, but the valley is a place that beckons again and again year round.

If you go out Route 30, the old Lancaster Pike, you will travel through the attractive Main Line suburbs. This gives you a chance to stop at old St. David's Church (Episcopal), built in 1715 and still used daily, as well as Waynesborough, the mansion home of the energetic revolutionary, Anthony Wayne (see text). The little stone church sits in a meadow surrounded by an extensive churchyard, where Wayne and other prominent people are buried. Longfellow as a visitor was so moved that he wrote a poem, which also can be seen. The church is on Valley Forge Road in the country near Wayne, Pennsylvania ((215)688-7947).

John Chadd was a young Quaker who ran the only ferry across the Brandywine in the 1700s. The house still stands near the battlefield at Chadds Ford on Route 100.

Nearby along the banks of the river is a renovated old mill, now the home of the Brandywine River Museum, which houses many of the original works of the entire Wyeth family. They have changing exhibitions, an excellent shop, a restaurant, and a courtyard where special events occur year round. You are welcome to picnic on the grounds in designated areas. Hours are from 9:30 a.m. to 4:00 p.m. daily except Christmas, and admission is required ((215)388-7601).

Kennett Square is named the "Mushroom Capital," and on Route 1 there is a small museum telling you some history and many, many ways for preparing mushrooms.

The Brandywine Battlefield, a state historical park, has the restored Washington's headquarters, a good introductory film, open ground on which you can ramble, and several seasonal events, among which are, of course, a recreation of the Battle of Brandywine by which the British gained access to Philadelphia while defeated Washington gathered his decimated troops at Valley Forge. No admission is required. Good picnicking exists under the tall trees where Washington and LaFayette conferred.

West of Route 1 is the Barnes-Brinton House, restored to its very unusual English-medieval architecture. Admission is required, and it is open June through August, Friday through Sunday, from 12:00 noon to 5:00 p.m. ((215)388-7376).

Longwood Gardens is one of the great estate gardens of the world and should not be missed even if you are not a garden enthusiast (see text for full information). Winterthur, grand estate of Henry Du Pont, is his unparalleled collection of 200 years of furnishings of decorative arts set in 196 rooms (see text for full information). Nemours mansion and its formal French gardens is the estate of another Du Pont, Alfred I. Set in 300 acres, the French chateau combines rare treasures with the life-style of the former resident. Located on Route 141 near Wilmington, Delaware, it is open for tours May through November, Tuesday through Saturday. Visitors must be over sixteen years of age, and admission is required ((302)651-6912).

The Delaware Art Museum has a collection of 150 years of American masterworks and changing exhibitions. You will see in the original Howard Pyle's familiar illustrations for Robin Hood and King Arthur. Located off Route 52 at 2301 Kentmere Parkway, Wilmington, Delaware, it is open Monday through Saturday from 10:00 a.m. to 5:00 p.m. and Sunday from 1:00 to 5:00 p.m. (admission).

The Delaware Museum of Natural History exhibits the state's natural flora and fauna in striking settings. It has one of the finest shell collections in the world, curated by Tucker Abbott, and you may walk across a beautiful barrier reef! It boasts a hall of mammals and a hall of birds among others. (For full information, see text.)

The Historical Society of Delaware has restored the Old Town Hall in Wilmington and has filled it with fascinating folk art. There are Delaware silver, toys, and an extraordinary doll's house. Across the way are six restored eighteenth-century houses (no admission required).

The Brandywine Valley is also conveniently close to New Castle, Annapolis, and Baltimore. You may find yourself continuing south!

Peruse the text for fuller information on designated sites and many more. At the Philadelphia Visitors Center, 15th and JFK Boulevard, ask for the folders "Discover Brandywine Valley" and "At Home in the Brandywine Valley." Both explain self-guided tours, and routes are easy to follow.

Routing: Take the Schuylkill Expressway west to Route 202 south. Follow Route 202 and exit at the Paoli Exit. Continue on 202 South which becomes Route 252 south after crossing Route 30. Exit at Route 1 and go south into the Brandywine Valley.

Notes

Notes

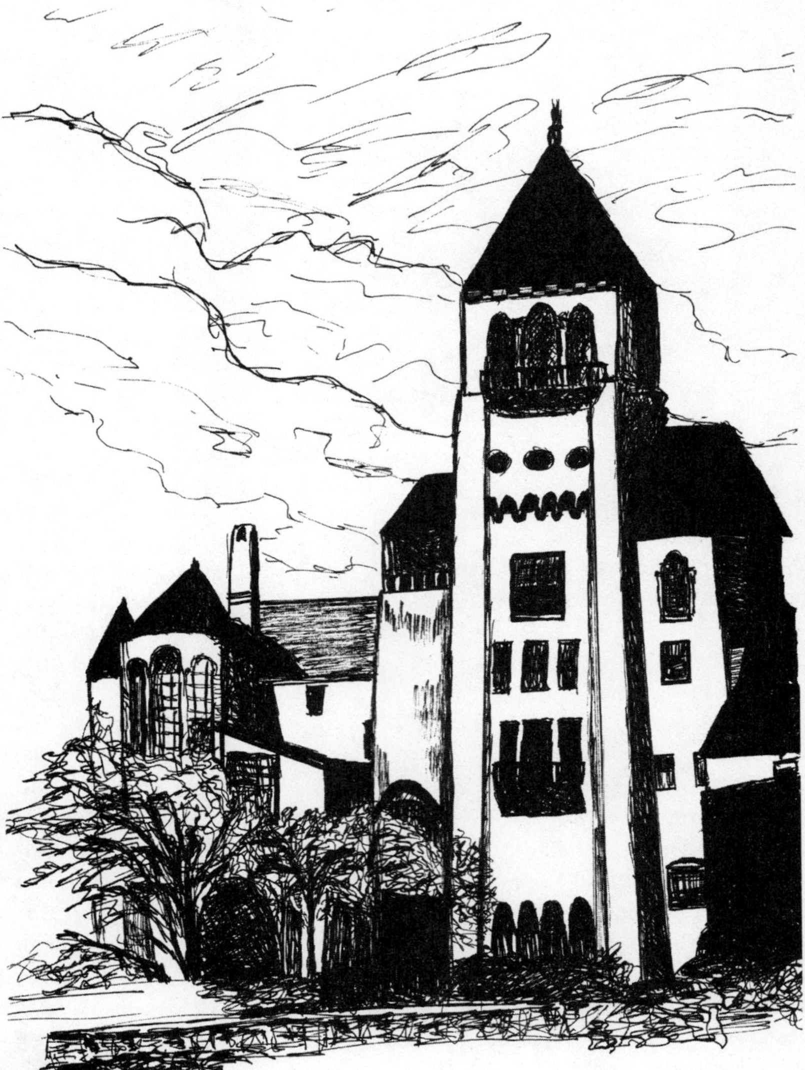
S.L. DeCurtis

Bryn Athyn

It is astonishing to find a large Gothic castle, a cathedral, and a surrounding village in rural Pennsylvania, but they were built to celebrate the Swedenborgian faith.

With wealth from both the Pennsylvania Railroad and Pittsburgh Plate Glass Company, Raymond Pitcairn relinquished the practice of law to devote many years to supervising this project himself. Artisans were dispatched to Europe to study the art of stained glass and brought home a formula further perfected in a large shop on the premises. More than one hundred stonemasons, carvers, and other artisans lived in the village surrounding the rising structures, working with only the best of materials. The spectacular gargoyles, stonework, and glass windows are the result of their devoted labor and skill. (In 1919 the cathedral was dedicated and is in constant use today.)

Glencairn, the Romanesque family house for his devoted wife and nine children, now houses floor after floor of the finest collection of twelfth and thirteenth-century stained glass and sculpture still in private hands. Rooms are filled with ancient treasures brought by Pitcairn to supply his assembly of Middle East and Mediterranean art, and it is hard to imagine little girls playing dolls or boys flying paper planes in the enormous 85-foot-high living room. Here are six beautiful reproductions of windows of Chartres Cathedral with two additional ones designed for the room. Above is a Musicians Gallery supported by stone gargoyles crafted to resemble each of his children with an instrument including a cigar-box banjo! Social and musical events were given regularly here to large invited audiences.

There are a quiet, enclosed cloister and a tall tower with an unusual firetiled roof at the top floor overlooking the peaceful rural valley and the Philadelphia skyline. Inside is the Pitcairn private chapel where some of the children were baptized. Its entrance doors bear a cross with the Alpha and Omega symbols, and its ceiling shows the four beasts of the Apocalypse. The library, once the master bedroom, with walls of dark teak, has treasures still being cataloged, including a reproduction of the beautiful Irish Book of Kells and a third-century Book of Manners, the original of which is housed at Trinity College, Dublin.

Shy, devoted, humorous Pitcairn died in 1966; and after his wife's death in 1979, Glencairn and its contents were given to the Academy of the New Church to be used as a cultural and community center. At 1001 Papermill Road off Huntingdon Pike, the Glencairn Museum is open by appointment Monday to Friday from 9:00 a.m. to 5:00 p.m. except for public holidays (215)947-9919 or -4200). Admission is required.

Routing: Go north on Broad Street to Route 611. Take Route 611 north and turn right on Route 63 (Old Welsh Road). Turn left onto Route 232 (Huntingdon Pike). Papermill Road is off the Pike in Bryn Athyn, Pennsylvania.

Notes

The Buten Museum

The name Wedgwood conjures up pretty blue and white pottery so popular with collectors. However, surprises will be awaiting you when you visit this museum. It is housed in the home built for pianist Josef Hoffman at 246 North Bowman Avenue, Merion Station, on the Main Line outside of Philadelphia. This was purchased by Harry Buten in 1931, who with his wife began their collection of Wedgwood. Their rare pieces and a scholar's research library were opened to the public in 1957 with more than 10,000 items on display. Among them are splendid examples of jasperware, lustrous pearlware, rosso antico, Parian ware, and majolica from early Josiah Wedgwood's time to 1984. A guide will explain the exhibits in the attractively furnished rooms. Jasperware may be the most familiar to you, and there is abundance of it to see. There is also the popular Victorian majolica with its varicolored glazes and imaginative designs. The enormous Alexander Vase, a five-foot creation hand-painted by Lesore, is a beauty and the largest Wedgwood ever made.

Wedgwood, who revolutionized pottery making in eighteenth-century England, had a rags-to-riches life story. A Renaissance man in talent and interests, this self-educated, liberal thinker was sympathetic to the Colonists during the Revolution and sent his own designed medallion against slavery to Benjamin Franklin. After years of perfecting his art, he opened a London gallery showroom, the first of its kind in the city. Wedgwood was named "Potter to the Queen" when the wife of King George III purchased his lovely creamware. This started an instant fashion that became known as "The Queen's Ware." Catherine the Great of Russia, not to be outdone, at once commissioned a set of 952 pieces! The Buten Museum contains three centuries of chess pieces, little rice spoons in the shape of a peacock's feather, basalt animals, and a footbath for the old plague, gout. Some of the loveliest

Wedgwood is the Moonlight Luster. There is also Fairyland Luster with its elves, fairies, imps, and leprechauns. Look for the amusing hedgehog designed to hold growing bulbs! Buten also acquired the letters and a complete set of Wedgwood catalogs from 1713 to the present. This is the only museum devoted solely to the popular Wedgwood and the history of its innovative creator.

Wedgwood ABC but NOT Middle E by Buten is the "bible" of collectors. His son David, curator of the collection in recent years, has also published several important books.

The museum in Buten's home is not hard to find and is interesting for its attractive floor plan and beautiful ironwork by Philadelphia master craftsman Sam Yellin. Call the museum first for tour information ((215)644-6601) and open hours.

You might make this a stop on your longer tour of the Main Line with visits to Bryn Mawr campus, a Friends' Meeting House, Waynesborough, and the Wharton Esherick Museum (see Main Line text).

Routing: Call first for exact street directions in Merion Station ((215)644-6601). To reach Merion Station take the Schuylkill Expressway to City Line (Route 1). Go south on Route 1. Turn right on Conshohocken Road (Route 23) and cross the railroad tracks. Do not follow Route 23 but proceed to Montgomery Avenue. Turn right on Bowman Avenue.

Notes

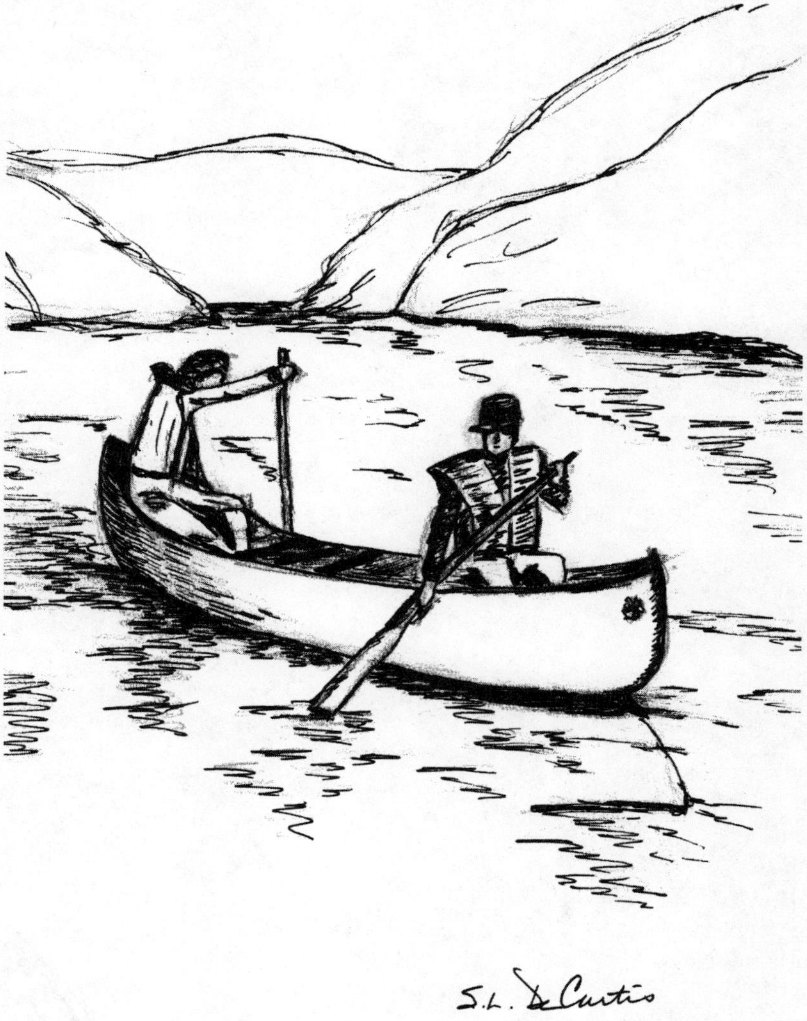
S.L. DeCurtis

Canoeing

To the enthusiasts the Great Outdoors is just that, great! And for those who revel in a day on quiet water, a lively romp over the rapids, or just the means of transportation for good bird-watching, the study of local flora or fauna, or a pleasantly slow route to a picnic, canoeing is a very pleasant answer. In the four states of Pennsylvania, New Jersey, Maryland, and Delaware, there are many places where you can leave the city far behind and, with your own canoe atop your car or in a good rental canoe, have a supreme day on some beautiful water. It has become a favorite pastime for hundreds of people, and the delight is growing annually.

If your idea of the Delaware River is one of oil tankers, overseas cargo vessels, and an occasional cruise liner putting into the Port of Philadelphia, we have news for you. The Delaware River is clear and beautiful from the New York Catskill Mountains to Trenton, New Jersey, and is one of the last scenic rivers in the East. Birds and small animal life still abound, particularly in early morning and at dusk. In the fall the autumn coloring is breathtaking, and you will feel like a Leni-Lenape Indian gliding quietly by cornfields, meadows, high cliffs, and woods.

In Upper Bucks County in Pennsylvania, Point Pleasant Canoe Rentals is the place to go for canoe rentals and information on group rentals for one- or two-day trips. The Delaware River here is so safe that Scout troops and grandmothers use it for weekend escapes! The canoes will not be birch bark or hollow logs but aluminum or, if you are going over the rapids, perhaps one of the new, flexible plastic canoes.

The Delaware Water Gap National Park offers Shawnee Canoe Trips from one hour to two weeks for either beginners or experienced canoe-campers. A firm briefing is given to all before you go out, and a waterproof map is provided showing rapids, etc. Their new videotapes should also be ready now. If you want to "shoot the rapids," Shawnee offers a daylong ticket so you can roar along Foul Rift and be picked up as often as you want.

At scenic Dingmans Ferry, Pennsylvania, Kittatinny Canoes has supplies of craft for overnight or shorter trips on the beautiful Delaware. It is a popular vacation spot, and you will find lots of friendly faces on quiet water for beginners or thrilling white water for those more adept. They have six bases over 125 miles of river and radio-dispatched vans to get you to one. They also have two good campgrounds with full facilities if that is your pleasure.

In the Pocono Mountain areas of Pennsylvania, another popular all-year-round vacationland (see text), there are many lakes, streams, and rivers that invite good canoeing. For those who like hustle and bustle, try Lake Wallenpaupack. You can happily combine this with a canoe trip on the Delaware or go rafting on Lehigh River white water.

In Delaware, Lum's Pond State Park has canoes as well as sailboats, paddleboats, or rowboats all for hire. And only one mile east of Laurel, Delaware, is Trap Pond State Park, which has a canoe trail through part of Great Cypress Swamp, the northernmost stand of natural bald cypress trees in the United States. It's like gliding into a primeval past for a day!

The Chester River Trail in Maryland is conveniently divided into three parts, each of which is an easy one-day adventure by canoe in good weather. (If the weather plays tricks, come ashore and walk about or bike through some of the interesting historic towns nearby.) Canoeists must put over their canoes only at a marina or a shore landing, as the remainder of the riverside is strictly private property. The canoe trail from Millington to Crumpton is a nice 6 miles; from Crumpton to Duck Neck Campground is another 4 miles; Duck Neck to Chestertown another 6 miles.

At the Chestertown Landing you will want to get off and visit this charming little town with its beautiful restored homes, main street stores, inns, and shops. Even before the Revolution this was a major port of entry as well as a safe landing for sailing vessels. Passengers en route to the Chesapeake Bay and further travel south were carried by overland stage, horse, wagon, or carriage to sail further down to James River plantations in Virginia with ports of call en route. Chestertown has a good Historical Society and good walking tour maps of the little town, which can be picked up at a bookstore. Just ask.

Millington, your starting place, was once the center of grain production in the eighteenth century with the old Higman Mill still standing. If you plan to canoe only from Millington to Crumpton on the narrow river, at this point you will see why the old rope ferry crossed here. There are many nice white houses in the small town if you want to stretch your legs.

These canoe trips are recommended for experienced canoeists, for there is no rescue service for overturned boats. However, contact the Tourism Council of Maryland for their excellent charter trips with a qualified guide who is also knowledgeable about local natural history and historic river life. Information and reservations should be made from TCUC in Stevenson, Maryland, the organization that supplies information about reputable canoe outfitters in Maryland and neighboring states. For advance information to plan a trip, write to this Tourism Council of the Upper Chesapeake at P.O. Box 66, Centreville, Maryland 21617, or call (302)758-2300. Ask for the simple, clear canoe trail map showing the points of interest and landings of the Chester River Trail.

In New Jersey across the Delaware, there is wonderful canoeing on the Batsto River in the Wharton Tract. Try the Bel Haven Canoe Rental (where you must make reservations). Their rate is low, but since they are very popular, they cannot accommodate walk-in rentals. From here you can canoe on many rivers; namely, the Batsto, Mullica, Wading, Oswego, Great Egg Harbor, or Maurice. Some routes take a few hours, some half a day, some a full day, some overnight, or some even a week. For the latter you must have a camping permit obtained from the Forest Office in Hammonton. Canoeists are driven to a drop-off point to find their own way downstream to a good stopping point. The Batsto River wanders, so keep a sharp eye out in your direction; but you will be rewarded by entering the lovely Batsto Lake at the end of your trip. Tie up and visit the restored village of Batsto, now deserted but once a thriving community where thousands worked at iron forges, glassmaking, and lumbering. Picnic areas are available (see text). For another good trip start at Hampton Furnace and go down to Lower Forge to camp for the night. Next day go on to Quaker Bridge. There are hiking trails in all this area, about which the ranger can tell you when you get your permit at the Ranger Office at the Batsto Visitors Center in the Lebanon State Forest.

Closer to Philadelphia is the lovely Brandywine River in Chester County, long a favorite waterway from Indian times to today. If it's rapids you want, start at Northbrook at Northbrook Canoe Rentals, which has a large fleet and half a dozen itineraries from Mortonville down to the rental area, just off Route 842 a couple of miles from West Chester, Pennsylvania.

Be extra careful in flash-flood season (particularly in April). The rental area closes when water reaches over dock level. In this season you may want to hike in the area or visit the famed Brandywine Museum on the riverbanks where the Wyeth family lives and paints. Nearby are the Brandywine Battlefields with explanatory films and lots to explore. Whatever your choice, the areas surrounding Philadelphia are easily and quickly reached for days outdoors, and you cannot go wrong whatever direction you choose to explore (see texts).

Pay a visit first to the Philadelphia Visitors Center at John F. Kennedy Plaza for the best routings to your selected place. If you belong to the AAA, they should be of help also. The Tourist Bureau can also supply you with necessary phone numbers in any of the nearby states.

Experienced canoeists know to bring along both warm-weather and rainy-weather clothing, a plastic bag in which to store wet clothing, a waterproof container for a camera, and shoes that can get really wet! Lotion and perhaps bug spray are also appreciated. If hot sun bothers you, bring a light, securely fitting hat and your sunglasses, of course. Leave valuables at home! Happy paddling in any of these areas!

Notes

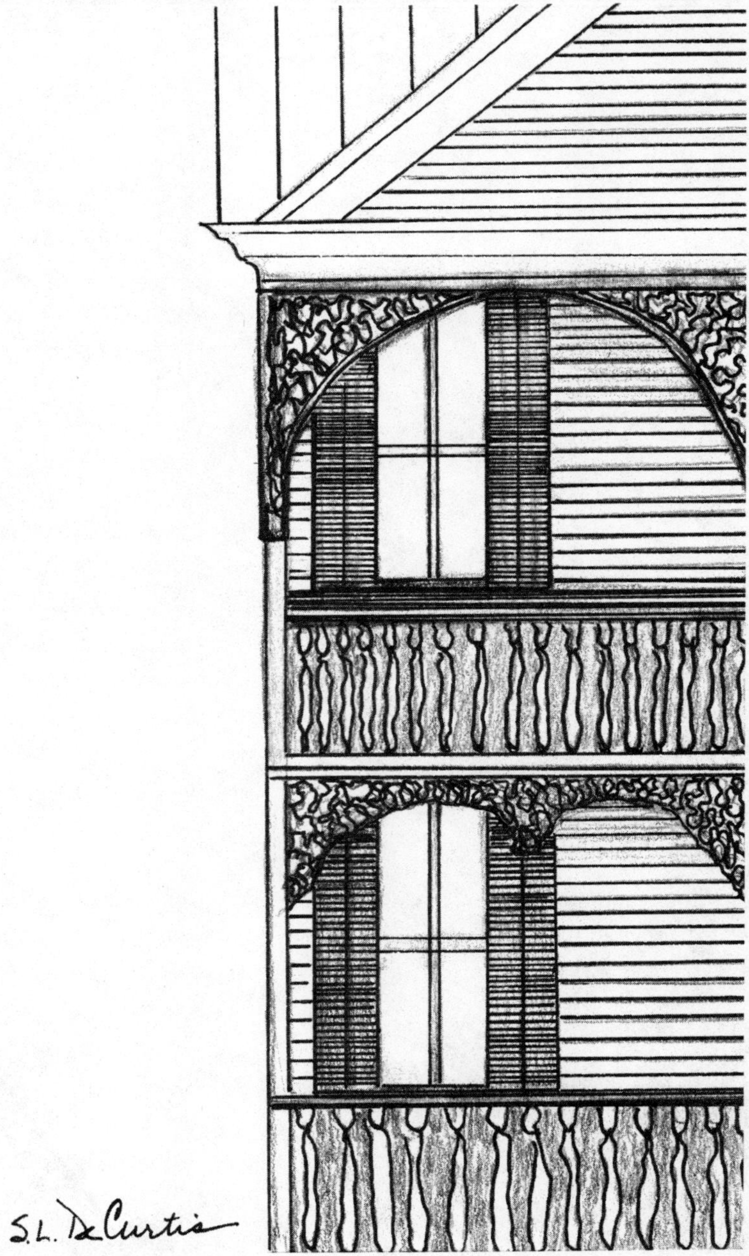
S.L. DeCurtis

Cape May

Once called Cape Island, this charming Victorian town is happily situated on the south New Jersey shore where the Delaware Bay empties into the Atlantic Ocean. It is seashore par excellence!

Its climate is sunny and breezy and in all seasons welcomes thousands of visitors. Even in winter its Victorian blocks of architecture draw students, architects, house renovators, art groups, and others studying "the real thing" in capsule.

In 1976 the town woke up to read that it was declared a National Historic Landmark and has thrived as such ever since.

Once the Leni-Lenape Indians roamed here harvesting fish and easily grown agricultural crops. Wild turkeys and other seasonal game were easily caught, and shellfish teemed along the shores. In 1630 the Dutch settled in the area and developed it as a whaling port. In the nineteenth century its climate beckoned Southerners who came by the Frenchtown and Newcastle Railroad to Delaware River steamboats to settle "at the shore" for blissful escape from the heat of Richmond, the Carolinas, and as far away as Georgia. With them came the Southern customs of ample meals, a leisurely pace, gentle manners, and a fashionable style rivaling that of Newport or Saratoga Springs.

By 1850, 3,000 visitors a day arrived to frequent the long boardwalks, rock on cool porches, or dance long into the summer nights with distinguished U.S. Presidents or the rich and socially prominent of three generations. Its several great hotels were booked far in advance, and spacious guesthouses on every block found room for large, happy families. "Cottages" in the fanciful designs favored by the newly rich were thrown up in composite style decorated with Valentine lacy scallops, whirls, and curlicues turned out by local carpenters from well-thumbed pattern books.

Today the streets are filled with strollers and cyclists gliding about

WEDGWOOD

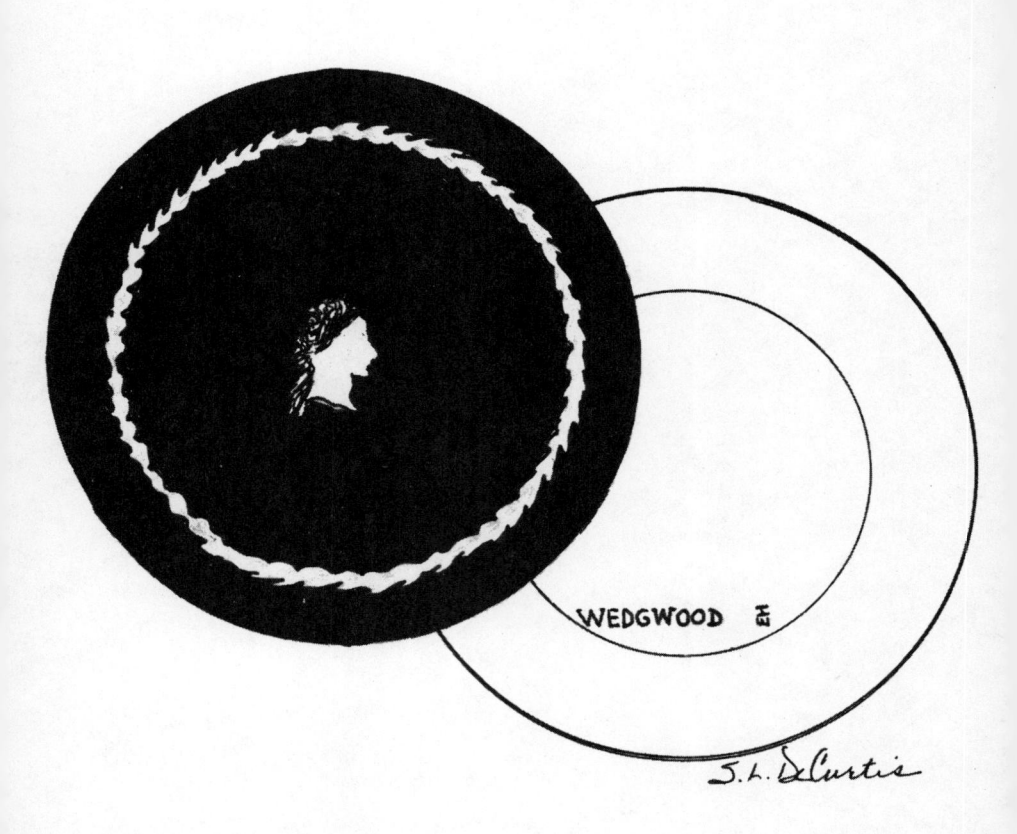

J. L. DeCurtis

the town to see the renaissance of these same summer homes large and small. The little trolley-bus tours are always popular for all ages. The beach is wide and good for swimming. Fishing reports come in daily to Philadelphia radio stations and *The Philadelphia Inquirer*. Restaurants abound at all prices. Sailing, swimming, and surfing are easy to enjoy, and there are always pretty girls to see. There are games and foods on the boardwalk and a venerable mechanical fortune-teller who is always correct!

Fall and winter holidays are especially popular with the well-filled Bed and Breakfast houses. Shops on the midtown mall remain open, and nearby Cape May Point Nature Preserve is busy with bird-watchers monitoring the flyway. In early October, Victorian Week is celebrated with house tours, lectures, a period fashion show, old-time vaudeville, and frequently an entire evening of costumed Gilbert and Sullivan. Christmas is beautifully festive with decorations, carols and choruses, and candlelight tours inside and out with the inns and homes hospitably open. There is also a special Charles Dickens tribute with readings and conviviality by the fireside. In late April and early May, thousands of early tulips bloom all over town for a weekend of Dutch dancing, foods, special art shows and classes, music, and horticultural sessions showing uses of tulips in a dozen ways.

From the Point you can have a long ferry ride across the bay to Lewes, the old town of the Delaware River pilots, and if you want the glamour of the Atlantic City casinos, they are an easy distance northward by car or bus. (Buses run on schedule to the casinos, believe it or not, from both Cape May and Lewes!)

Plan to spend a full day and perhaps a night at Cape May, for you will see a tranquil history of the past still in the making.

Routing: Go south on Broad Street to Route 76. Take Route 76 east and cross over the Walt Whitman Bridge. Follow signs to the Atlantic City Expressway and take the expressway to the Garden State Parkway exit. Go south on the Garden State Parkway to Cape May.

Notes

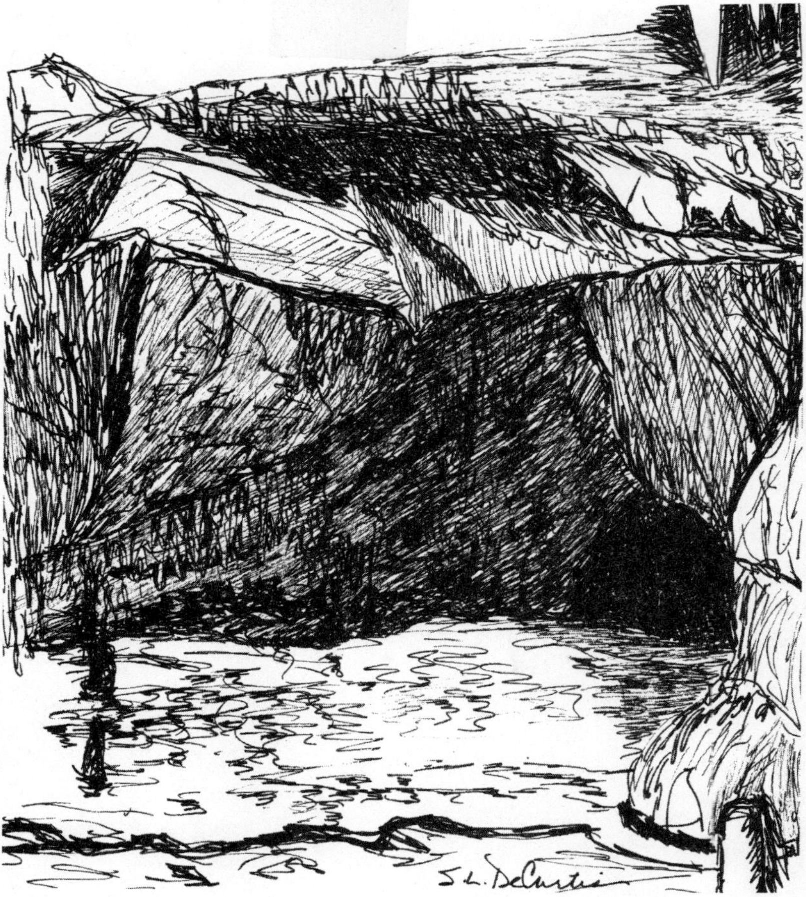
S.L. DeCurtis

Caves and Caverns

Underground passageways, rooms, grottoes, and caverns are endlessly fascinating. Walk a rocky trail or go by boat into chambers hidden for centuries, recalled only by persistent legends of Indian burial grounds with mystic ceremonies by subterranean lakes, great stalactites, and colorful stalagmites.

Pennsylvania is honeycombed with caves and caverns beneath woodland and mountain Indian trails. Here great underground rivers have flowed through soft limestone for thousands of years. Seepage water or a single drop are now riverbeds far below the earth, their flow carrying minerals, silt, and stones on long journeys. These lodge in narrow crevasses to form barriers that through the ages collect roughage or release more minerals from the limestone rock. Streams have turned into underground palaces of great beauty now revealed under electric light. Huge pillars, buttresses, and fantastic shapes resemble cathedrals, animals, arches, or bridges across gurgling water that disappears into silent, dark tunnels. These caverns have been well explored for years, and safe walkways with guardrails have been installed. Lights shine on or behind these wonders so that you can see for yourself this colorful, mysterious underworld. Some of the best operated and most interesting are listed, and you will probably find literature on more as you go along.

Indian Echo Caverns, 3 miles west of Hershey, Pennsylvania, is off Route 322 at Hummelstown. Massive columns created by slowly dripping waters were discovered before the Revolution. This is land of the Susquehannock Indians, who undoubtedly knew it well. It was also the home of a hermit, Amos Wilson, who lived here with a broken heart. The caverns are open from 9:00 a.m. to 6:00 p.m. Memorial Day to Labor Day, and from 10:00 a.m. to 4:00 p.m. in April, May, September, and October. (In March and November they are open weekends only.) There are an Indian Trading Post and large picnic grounds and room for small children to roam. Write P.O. Box 206, Hummelstown, Pennsylvania 17036 ((717)566-8131). The caverns are situated 10 miles east of Harrisburg and 3 miles west of Hershey and Hershey Park.

Crystal Cave near Kutztown, Pennsylvania, on Route 222, is in the heart of the Amish country. It got its name from the milky white natural columns. Ceilings of breathless beauty are lighted, and on the 45-minute guided trip you will see the Giant's Tooth, the Totem Pole, the Ear of Corn, and the Tobacco Leaves. There are also a Natural Bridge and a magnificent Cathedral Chamber. Discovered in 1871, it has had thousands of visitors, who start with the slide presentation "Inside the Earth" and then go on a tour. There are 25 acres of nature walks with farm animals and Indian tepees to see. Picnicking is welcomed in their grove. For full information write Crystal Cave, R.D. #3, Kutztown, Pennsylvania 19530 ((215)838-8767).

At Hellertown, 2 miles south of Bethlehem, Pennsylvania, there is a cave with the romantic name of Lost River Cavern. This wonderland of crystal shapes has five separate chambers and an underground river that takes its own place in history. See the Natural History Rock and the Mineral Museum and you will have a better understanding of the world in which mankind is only a recent participant. There are also an indoor tropical garden and a place for picnics. Guided tours leave every half hour ((215)838-8767).

For a full day's trip go west to Penn's Cave, one of the most popular caverns since 1885. Wear a jacket or a sweater for the 45-minute boat ride that glides from room to room and dusty gray color to brilliant scarlet. You will come out on the Indian Lake Nitanee where the light of day may dazzle your eyes. The cave is open year round, and at a nearby airport there are also scenic plane rides. Ask about them. For a Penn's Cave folder write Centre Hall, Pennsylvania 16828.

If you are a cave nut or want to become one, you should know about the National Speleological Society dedicated to the preservation of caves and caverns. Their Philadelphia branch is called the Philadelphia Grotto and meets regularly each month at the University of Pennsylvania in Philadelphia with other branches in Newark, Delaware; Bucks County; and York, Pennsylvania. Their motto is, "Take nothing but pictures, leave nothing but footprints, and kill nothing but time."

There are explorers and guides for groups from seven to fifty-one of either new or seasoned spelunkers. They have done mapping and surveying and have ventured into caves where no other person has stood.

No two caves are alike, varying from formations as delicate as a spider's web to giant rock formations. They have viewed underground waterfalls and silent lakes millions of years old and have studied the fossil remains of prehistoric animals on the cliffsides.

Caves and caverns are a lure for all ages and can remind us all of man's very recent introduction to this planet. The Philadelphia Visitors Bureau at 15th and JFK Boulevard ((215)568-6599) should have folders for you and can give you quick routings to a day's adventures underground.

Notes

Chestnut Hill

A leisurely day in this attractive suburb can give you an added perspective on how some Philadelphians live.

Affluent Colonial citizens left the city's hot summer for "clearer airs and fresher waters" of nearby Germantown with the most affluent going out farther into what is now Chestnut Hill. It was during the great yellow fever epidemic that Washington and many of his aides removed themselves and their families to this area to escape the mounting death toll.

At the close of the Civil War and the construction of the Pennsylvania Railroad two local far-sighted men, Henry Houston and George Woodward, planned an entire small community to attract year round residents. The lure, of course, was the new fast form of transportation successfully accomplished by Alexander Cassatt across the river on the Main Line.

For the past two centuries the Great Road from Germantown to Philadelphia was a major artery for farmers and manufacturers bringing food and wares to town. The new railroad was to be constructed beyond it to the top of a hill crowned with lovely chestnut trees.

This planned village very soon contained new schools, churches, a summer hotel, and benefited from the services of gardeners, grooms, maids, nurses, and coachmen. Comfortable fieldstone houses designed as twin or single dwellings were built to resemble Welsh cottages with peaked roofs, casement windows, wide fireplaces, and in the English manner, a comfortable upstairs living room. Interior woodwork was of the best quality and outside airy porches invited family gatherings. Local Chestnut Hill stone gives them all a most substantial appearance and some uniformity.

Smaller houses were built for the servant staff as even larger estates were designed and built, reaching out into the deep countryside where handsome Georgian estates already stood in cool parks.

Today the city trolley runs the length of Germantown Avenue, the spine of this community, to the very top of "the Hill." Former houses have been turned into offices or specialty shops, book and toy stores, service buildings, flower shops, galleries, banks, and hardware stores. There are still some butcher shops where they still cut to order. The second hand shops are frequented by antique dealers, and a consortium of pediatricians is placed wisely near an ice cream shop!

If you are driving you can park in any of the community parking lots, and if you are making a purchase, you can get your parking ticket stamped entitling you to free parking. The area is so compact and attractive for browsing that you will find this is the best plan.

The restored, old drovers' hotel has guest rooms and a restaurant inside as well as outside for dining on the porch. Behind it is the Farmers Market which is the hub for neighborly weekend shopping.

Over the crest of "the hill" and beyond the hospital is the Woodmere Gallery of decorative arts. Once the home of a wagon driver turned millionaire, it specializes in works of Delaware Valley artists. It is open without charge Tuesday through Saturday from 10:00 a.m. to 5:00 p.m. ((215)247-0476). It also has an attractive gift shop.

Beyond this gallery is the beautiful Morris Arboretum with several magnificent gardens and ponds. This is most inviting for a quiet stroll after a warm day and the seasonal flower and tree displays are delightful. There is often a special event taking place that you can enjoy such as kite flying, morris dancing, etc.

The entire Chestnut Hill area is made for camera bugs with intriguing shots of turreted houses, galleries, tall windows, lacy ironwork, cupolas, spires, and port-cocheres which give good contrast to the sturdier Welsh homesteads of the village.

If you are driving be sure to turn left over "the Hill" at Bell's Mill Road (Woodmere is on one corner) and descend to Wissahickon Creek. Park there, for no cars are allowed on Forbidden Drive which is given over to walkers, horseback riders, joggers, bikers, and fishermen. Follow the stream by the path (turn to your left) and you will come to a tall wooden Indian commemorating the Delaware Indians who once used this pretty area as a summer camping ground. No wonder! There are also an old tavern, ducks to feed, and places to picnic.

Chestnut Hill is an informal town as interesting as Georgetown outside of Washington, D.C. People chat on the street, and there are community street fairs, parades, outdoor plant sales, and a charming spring flower show using the windows of shops lining Germantown Avenue as showcases. In the fall the Independence Marathon runs right through the town and on to Independence Hall, so you can cheer the runners on.

Chestnut Hill offers a good, leisurely day of exploring either by car or on foot after you have alighted from the Chestnut Hill local from the railroad station at Penn Center.

It is a good combination with Hope Lodge and Peter Wentz Farm both farther out in the country (see text).

Routing: Take the Benjamin Franklin Parkway to Kelly Drive. Turn onto Wissahickon Drive and follow to the Lincoln Drive. Continue on Lincoln Drive and turn right on Allen's Lane and follow to Germantown Avenue. Take Germantown Avenue to Chestnut Hill.

Chestnut Hill local trains run about every half hour from Penn Center Station located at 17th Street and JFK Boulevard.

Notes

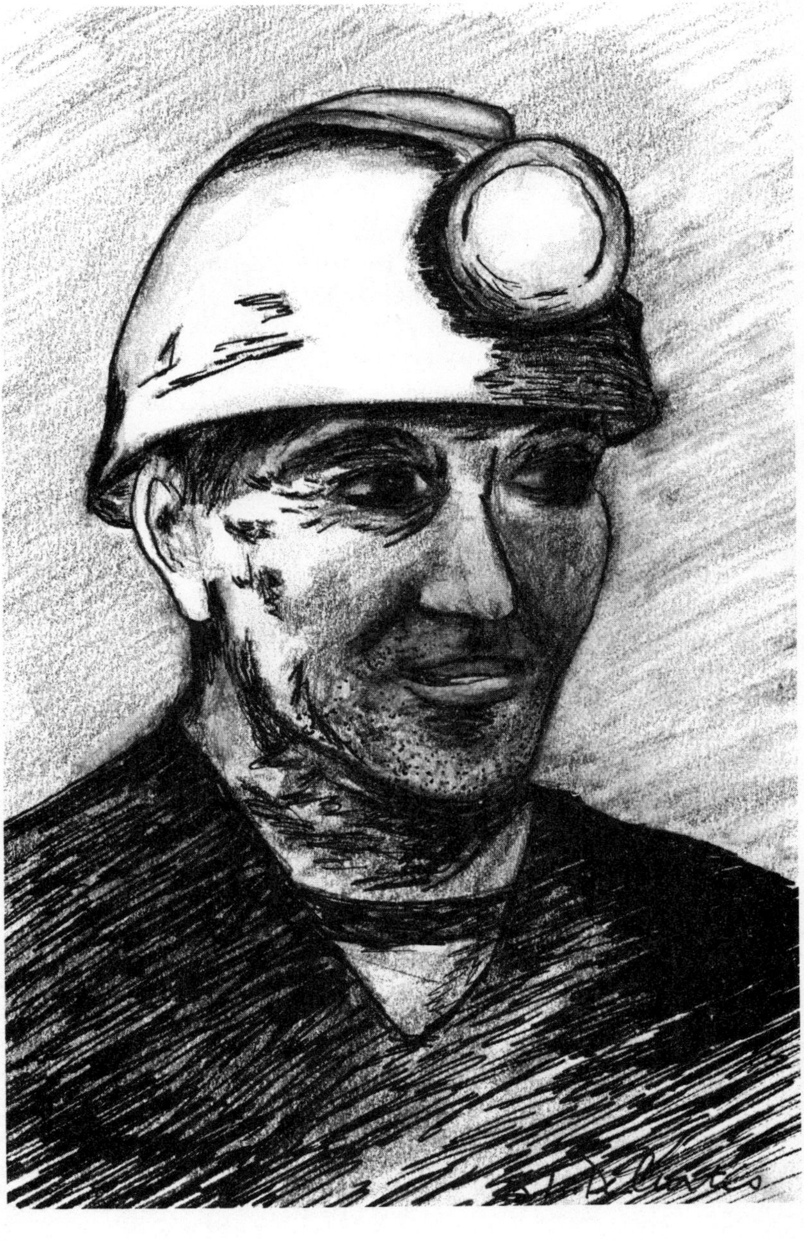

Coal Mine Adventure

The "black diamond" riches networking Pennsylvania are the great coal mines under the highways and cities of today. For decades coal fired great steel furnaces and tiny forges and warmed homes and stores before the advent of electric heat. Townspeople were almost all miners, and mines so prosperous before and after the Civil War and the turn of the century now lie forgotten, dying, and, in many cases, hopeless.

Great canals transported the fuel to the river ports of Kingston, Port Jervis, Philadelphia, or New York in a constant procession. Long coal-laden barges were a common sight on the navigable rivers that led to the great bays or the sea.

The lively life of canal towns is only a memory now for busy railroad towns supplanted them and they too have vanished in history. But you can still go underground and see a real coal mine!

There is an actual horizontal drift mine in Ashland, Pennsylvania, where you can don weatherproof jackets, board a genuine jitney train used formerly by the miners, and travel deep below the surface into a long-active mine. Closed for many years, the mine shaft is now open to tourists and made safe year round. The average underground temperature is about 50 degrees and some seepage of water may drip from overhead so bring a sweater, a hat, or a scarf. Wear rubber-soled shoes if you can, for you will walk underground, led by an experienced guide. Pioneer Tunnel runs for 1,800 feet deep into the side of Mananoy Mountain, and after this visit you will understand the terrible hazards and exhausting labor required of miners who spent their lives there.

At the Administration Building in Ashland Pioneer Mine, buy your ticket in a room that was formerly the colliery office. You will board a yellow train with three open cars running on a single track under a line of electric lights. This lighting did not exist in old mining days, for then there were only the little lamps worn on the front of miners' caps to guide them. They stood all day on "bottom rock" with "top rock" overhead as they hacked and pulled chunks of coal from the veins that ran between. A few hand-held lanterns may have cast flickering glows as they worked to load the chunks on the cars that hauled the coal to the surface. They were pulled by mules who never saw the light of day. Once outside, the coal was carried by steam train to a "washing station" before it was loaded into the barges going downriver.

Before veins of coal could be mined, deep shafts and the long "galleries" must first by tunneled out (many by hand), then shored up with mammoth beams, logs, and ladders all carried on the shoulders of the miners, who must also set them firmly in place and hope for no cave-ins! The galleries often honeycombed the depths of the mountains for miles with the damp atmosphere reeking with acid, corrosive water. The only fresh air to come down from the surface was through small ventilators, which the miners themselves must also construct in a shaft-like design.

The Pioneer Tunnel of Ashland has a remarkable safety record, unlike many others, for in its fifty years of operation supplying coal to fifty states and fifty-eight foreign countries, it never had an accident. When you surface after almost an hour in these dark, damp depths, you will want to visit the nearby Anthracite Museum of tools, displays, machinery, and models. If the "Steam Lokie" is running that day, you can have a thirty-minute ride around Manahoy Mountain and see the "bootleg hole" dug by some miners trespassing and eager to pull a few sacks of coal up to sell or to use themselves.

Pioneer Tunnel is open daily from May 30 to Labor Day. The tunnel closes at 4:00 p.m. the Saturday before Labor Day for an annual Ashland Boys' Association event. During May, September, and October it is open Saturday and Sunday. Write ahead for up-to-date information to Ashland Community Enterprises, 19th and Oak streets, Ashland, Pennsylvania 17912 or phone (717)875-3850.

Routing: Go west on the Schuylkill Expressway to the Pennsylvania Turnpike. Take the turnpike west to Exit 22. Follow signs to I-176 (to Reading). Take I-176 north to Route 422. Follow Route 422 north to Route 222. Go north on Route 222. Turn left (north) at Route 61 and follow to Ashland. There will be Pioneer Tunnel signs in that town.

Notes

Amish Country

A Day in the Amish Country

Though they are frequently called the Pennsylvania Dutch, these hardworking farmers of the fertile Lancaster Valley are truly Germans who came to this country from the Palatine region of towns bordering on the Rhine River.

Religiously persecuted after the Thirty Years War of 1619 to 1648, they found new doors opened to them by the young English missionary William Penn, who preached love and tolerance for all faiths and nations. Under King Louis XIV the Edict of Nantes decreed that all children must be educated as Catholics. After their villages and farms were confiscated or laid waste, hundreds of these beleaguered families fled first to benevolent Holland and then boarded ships to the New World.

Superb and energetic farmers, these staunch believers in individual liberty set up small, clannish colonies here to reaffirm their old customs of strict honesty, hard work, and large families. Refusing to use modern inventions such as electricity, machinery, cars, or trucks, they still farm with horse and plow. They do not mingle socially or intermarry with the "English," which is their name for outsiders. Education of the young stops at thirteen, when both boys and girls augment the dawn-to-dark labor. Constantly industrious, the Amish have built up many respected businesses in regional Farm Markets as far as 75 miles away. Here they daily sell their own butchered meats, bakery goods, dairy products, vegetables, and Amish specialties. The stalls are run by young girls demurely dressed in plain, dark, modest dresses with delicate white organdy caps tied primly on their heads. Cosmetics and jewelry are taboo. Strict attention to duty is the word, and the elders keep close supervision on the young! Because farmland is rapidly diminishing and prices for new tracts are beyond their economic reach, some younger Amish have "broken," earning them the nickname of "black bumpers," since they drive cars, wear jogging shoes on tired feet, and have entered some of the building trades.

The Amish population, of which there is no accurate count, has spread into Ohio, Indiana, upstate New York, and Canada, where they are buying land that has deteriorated or fallowed. Slowly they are again rebuilding and farming in their constant, predictable manner.

A drive through the Lancaster Valley along the old Lancaster Pike (Route 30) shows their beautiful, neat farms. You will undoubtedly see their shiny little black buggies pulled by a high trotting horse as they go on their way to church. Here the sexes separate to converse separately after a service that includes much singing. The young people find their only social life in the "evening singing" or in the community assistance in the large projects of barn building, house repairs, etc.

Courting for a wedding is private and quiet, for the young man must first go to a deacon of the church and appeal to him to approach the intended's father for permission to marry her. Banns are published, and the old-style wedding, though joyous, is solemn and simple. Tradition is observed in an abundant feast prepared and served by the women, accompanied by more singing. Games follow played by boys and men while the women either settle down to talk or go for quiet walks. After a week the couple visits each guest at the wedding and receives a gift. Since both boys and girls receive presents from birth to furnish a household when they eventually move from father's house, their new homes are well equipped.

There is an Information Center off Route 30, plainly marked, where you can find Amish homesteads. Here you may visit a working farm and have ample, homestyle meals. There are many Farmers Markets selling their apple butter, sticky buns, pickled eggs, sausage, and beautiful fruits and vegetables. You won't be able to resist and will probably buy a local basket to carry it all!

Souvenirs abound, but for the more serious there are antique shops, basket shops, wooden wares, painted tinware, and the beautiful Amish quilts that fetch hundreds of dollars.

Not far away is the Strasburg Railway, where you can ride through the countryside for a fare ticket. Along one side is a wonderful Railroad Museum, where there are handsome engines on display (see Railroading text). In the nearby town of Lititz is the Wilbur Chocolate Factory, where you can watch the candy process of hand-dipping and see their exhibits of chocolate pots and other European wares (no admission). The town of Columbia also has the popular Wilton Armetalware house, where you can see the art of metal sandcasting Mondays through Fridays. If you are a seamstress, the Columbia Garment Factory is for you with 10,000 ribbons, laces, findings, buttons, trims, and fabrics (see text for Wright's Ferry Mansion).

The towns of Lancaster and York, named for those English towns of the War of the Roses, have much history in their well-restored buildings and walking tours. Colonial York was for more than a year the capital of the country when the English took over Philadelphia. The Founding Fathers thought it wise to drive their carriages swiftly up Lancaster Pike with the state papers and themselves (see texts). You are also not far from Gettysburg, which remembers that grim battle of the Civil War in a National Park with films, markers, and a trail that can be easily followed. The Eisenhower Farm is also nearby (see text).

There are many places to stay if you decide to extend your visit, which is a good plan if you are anxious to really absorb both the Amish country and Gettysburg. No visit to Philadelphia is complete without a day spent in this beautiful, old-world place where quiet pleasures and industrious farming are the backbone of a rural life only a short trip away.

Routing: Go west on the Schuylkill Expressway. Exit at City Line Avenue (Route 1) and go south. Turn right onto Route 30 (Old Lancaster Pike). Proceed directly to Lancaster, Pennsylvania. It is well marked. Alternatively, for a faster route take the Schuylkill Expressway to Route 202 and go south on Route 202 to the Route 30 exit. Proceed west on Route 30 to the Downingtown Bypass. Take the bypass and continue west on Route 30 into Lancaster and continue west.

Notes

Notes

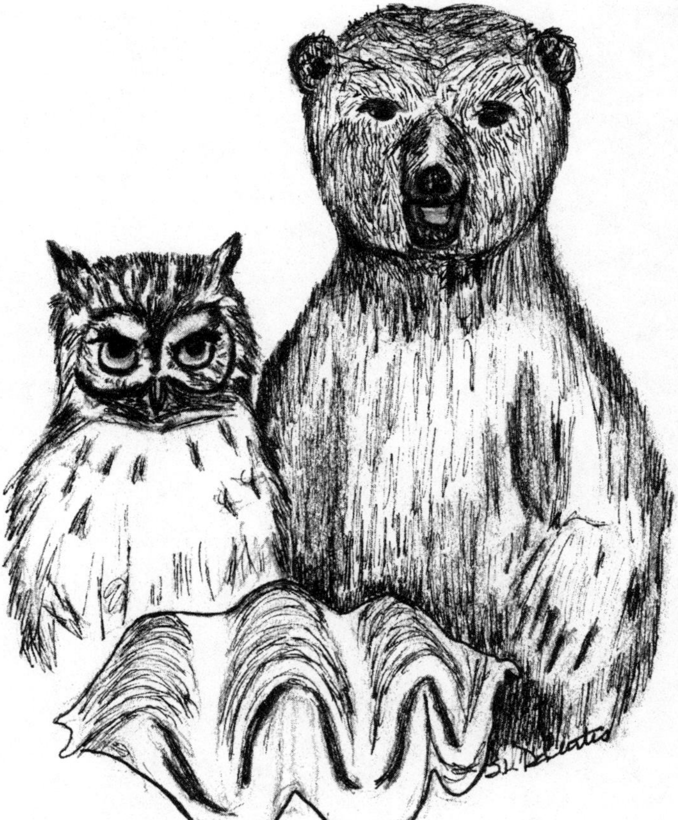

Delaware Museum of Natural History

This excellent museum, visited by 30,000 people each year, is situated in Greenville, 5 miles northeast of Wilmington, Delaware, and is easily found on Route 52 (also called Kennett Pike).

Because of its subject interest and proximity it would make a good one-day visit, including the Brandywine Museum in Chadds Ford, Pennsylvania (see text). They also have developed an active Conservancy Program, and around the museum there are marked nature trails, many specimens of flowers, ferns, bushes, and trees, and, of course, the Brandywine River, which is monitored for good canoeing.

The Delaware Museum is devoted to the theme of "Sky, Land, and Sea," emphasizing the Delaware Valley terrain and its inhabitants. There are 131 exhibits, including mammals, birds, and shells found in this area and other parts of the world. Other important exhibits from the South Seas have also been included. You will be able to walk across a coral reef set into the floor so you can peer through the sea grasses to see marine life as though you were snorkeling. This was designed by the eminent C. Tucker Abbot, whose books you know if you are a shell enthusiast.

Throughout history shells have played an important role with many uses in religion, as tools, as money, and as ornaments. Examine the intricate shell embroidery perfected by the North American Indian with their special jewel-like designs and artistry.

Shellfish are part of the great chain of life for man and other inhabitants of this planet. They have long been a source of income also for the Delaware watermen, and their decrease is of particular concern to this region. The clear trumpet call on a conch shell is still used by fishermen in the Caribbean and Mediterranean to signal a change of weather, a great catch, or a meeting. This loud carrying sound is used in a natural way, much like the signal uses of bonfires or smoke.

Museum dioramas show the cliffs where eagles nest, and an East African water hole with beasts coming down to drink at dawn or dusk. You can study the history of the now-extinct passenger pigeon, whose dense, migratory flocks once darkened skies for miles. You will see marsh birds, birds of the North Atlantic Sea Cliff, and the strange birds of New Zealand. (For local bird-watching in nearby areas, see The Great Outdoors in text.)

One of the most unusual and lovely exhibits is that showing the use of feathers throughout the ages. Note particularly the great royal cloaks in splendid colors created by the Pacific Ocean inhabitants.

There is the life of a Delaware stream depicting the day of a busy otter, a mink, and a sentinel bluejay.

A Delaware woodland is nearby with graceful white-tailed deer often seen each fall in local cornfields. There are also handsome skunk, perky cottontails, little tufted titmice, and a pileated woodpecker searching for insects on a tree trunk. His scarlet toque is the only accent in his skillful camouflage of dusky black-and-white dress.

The Delaware Museum offers a full range of programs and is also home to many groups for meetings. Its special events include a Discovery Room where children and adults come on Sundays to see small animals while learning about their life and habits. Natural history films are shown several times daily, so inquire at the entry desk for showings Wednesdays through Sundays.

The attractive museum shop maintains good prices for all ages and interests.

The museum is open Tuesday through Sunday from 9:30 a.m. to 4:30 p.m. and Sunday from 12:00 noon to 5:00 p.m. Admission is required ((302)652-7600).

Routing: Take the Schuylkill Expressway west to City Line (Route 1). Go south on Route 1 through Chadds Ford. Turn left on Route 52. The Delaware Museum of Natural History is on the right.

Notes

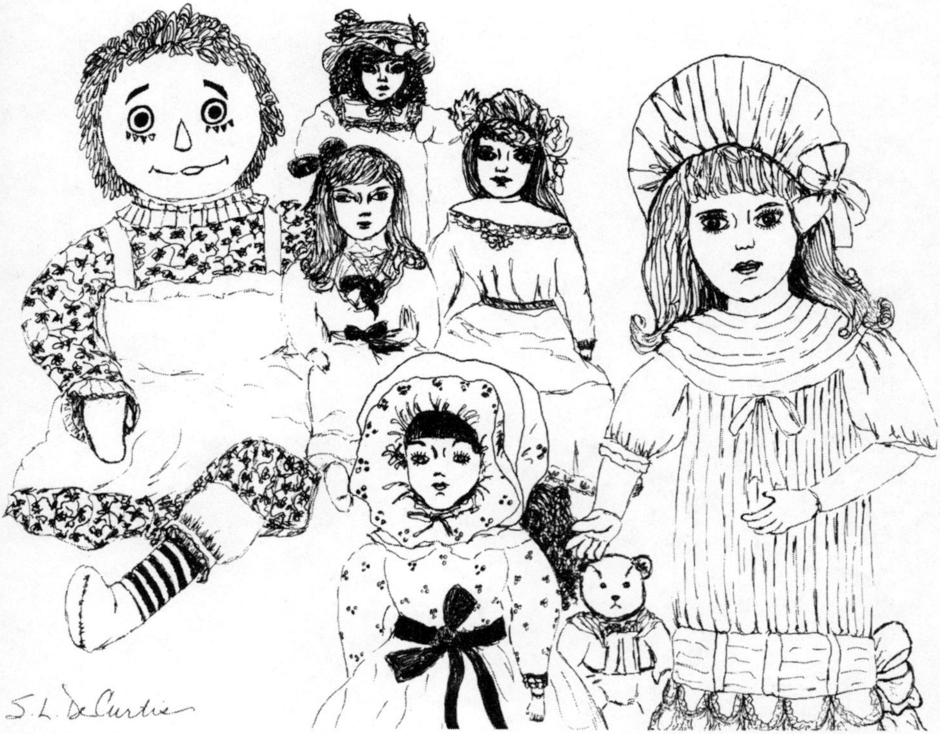
S. L. DeCurtis

Dolls, Dolls, Dolls!

Dolls have been used universally as toys, religious symbols, portrayers of fashion, and a means of advertising. Collectors world round love them, old and new, and so does every little girl who wants to play house. Dolls are carried to college rooms by their young owners, give comfort in strange hospital rooms, and sometimes serve for angry spankings when all the world seems wrong to a three-year-old's eyes.

One of the greatest collections of all kinds of dolls, more than 2,500 from a collection of 5,000, is on view in Douglassville, Pennsylvania, near Pottstown. In Mary Merritt's cases, fabulous dolls are set against fabrics, fans, or furnishings of every period. Many are exceedingly rare, such as the tiny leather-faced street peddlers carrying miniature trays of wares! There are character dolls, dolls with beeswax faces, some with fine porcelain heads, papier-mache dolls with leather bodies, wooden dolls, and seven tiny wax dolls dressed as children of the old London Foundling Hospital.

There are dolls in native dress, dolls scaled to the several wonderfully furnished dollhouses, baby dolls asleep and awake, familiar rag dolls, and Pennsylvania Dutch dolls that can be flipped over to reveal small animals beneath their skirts that were used to cast spells on beasts and for local powwow healings. Since many sects in the Lancaster area did not approve of "graven images," their little girls played with faceless, fully clothed dolls. Many of you will remember your Frozen Charlotte doll and her Parisian bisque face or the German dolls with china heads from the town of toys, Nuremberg. As these were not made on modern production lines, each doll had her own individual face. Some were made to resemble popular famous persons such as Jenny Lind, Empress Eugenie, or Queen Victoria.

After 1880 fashion dolls were dressed not in grown-up clothes in small size but in childlike apparel. Monsieur James heads the list of artist doll-makers using human hair, glass rather than painted eyes, and very alert expressions. These charming creatures are fascinating in their detail of authentic dresses, bonnets, capes, or hats. When you have absorbed these rooms full of dolls and the several dollhouses furnished in complete detail, go next door to their museum of "collectables."

Farther afield on Route 73 in the town of Skippack is Shirley Kasum's Nostalgia House in West Chestnut Hill or Roxanne LeMay's shop on Haws Lane in Flourtown where, by appointment, she runs a doll hospital and makes rag dolls and super doll clothes. If you are farther afield in the Amish country, visit Der Sonder Haus in the town of Bird-In-Hand. In Chester County, Pennsylvania, Richard Wright, known internationally as a dealer in dolls, is housed in a 200-year-old farmhouse in Birchrunville at the corner of Flowing Springs and Hollow Roads.

Doll shows and sales are listed almost weekly in the What-To-Do Weekend Section of *The Philadelphia Inquirer*. Everyone interested in dolls waits to see the amusing Christmas exhibition of Wyeth dolls "at play" at the Brandywine Museum. (Consult the papers for dates.) Sometimes they are outdoors skating in a woodland setting; sometimes they are having a tea party. They are a cherished collection, and you will love them too. (The men and boys may hang around wonderful rooms of running model trains filling two large galleries!)

Collector or enjoyer, you will find many places to see and find dolls but a fine place to start is the Mary Merritt Museum. It is open daily from 10:00 a.m. to 5:00 p.m., Sundays and holidays ((215)-385-3809).

Routing: Take the Schuylkill Expressway west to the Pennsylvania Turnpike. Follow the turnpike west to Exit 23 (Route 200). Go north on Route 100 to U.S. 422 and go west. The Mary Merritt Museum, which is well marked, is on the right about 1 mile.

Notes

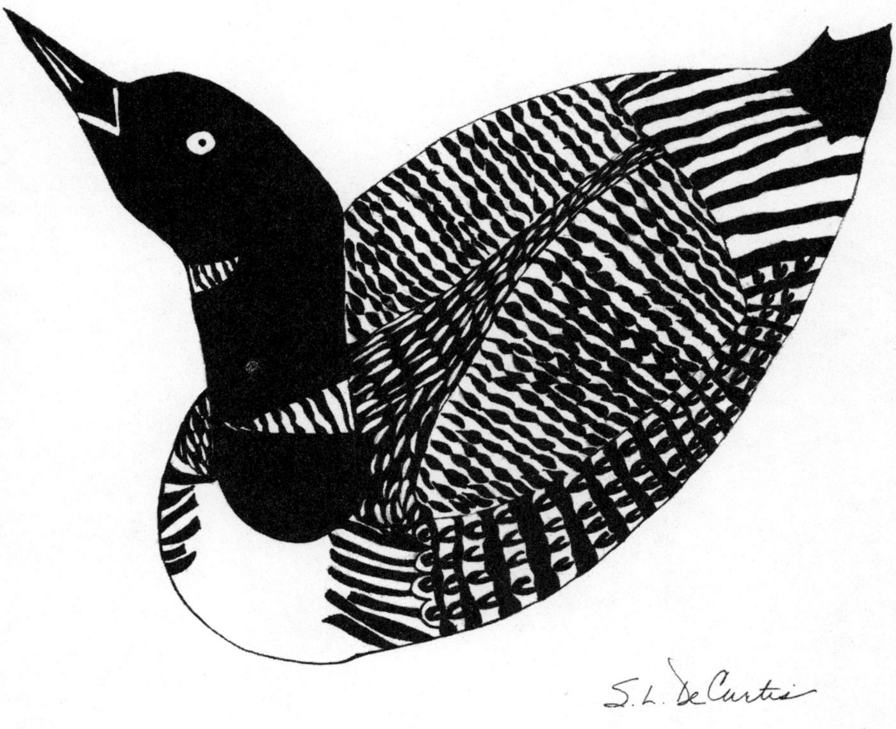
S. L. DeCurtis

The Eastern Shore

We Americans have nicknames for large areas. When we refer to The Coast, we know it means only the west coast of the United States. The Cape means Cape Cod, not Cape Ann or Cape Canaveral. The Eastern Shore (not to be confused with just the plain shore of the New Jersey seaside) is the east coast of the enormous Chesapeake Bay. No trip to Philadelphia is complete without a leisurely day or two exploring this nearby section of Maryland and Delaware, which has quite a different life-style and appearance from those of the Main Line, Chestnut Hill, the Amish country, or the coal region.

Colonial New Jersey towns do not have the slightly southern ambiance of the Eastern Shore! Its ragged coastline is filled with little villages, old forts, cities whose citizens for three centuries shaped America, and, of course, that magnificent and historic body of water, Chesapeake Bay, known locally as The Bay.

European explorers of the 1600s sailed those waters mapping the New World and believing this to be a vast inland sea. Here mast builders later designed the Baltimore clippers and crafted the famed Skipjacks for the working watermen's needs. Its people are a combination of English, French, Scots, Germans, and, lately, some Asiatics who have farmed the fertile soil, traded on the rivers and The Bay, transported goods and chattel for households north and south, and turned the waterwheels of the mills around the countryside.

Several large rivers pour into The Bay and course through it today, and its islands, peninsulas, coves, and little harbors are favorites with yachtsmen from all over the world. The long Chesapeake Bay Bridge Tunnel, built after World War II, opened it to land travelers, who now relish the seasonal game hunting across its fields and marshes; the wide variety of fishing; its historic houses, galleries, and churches; handsome estates; antiques; and always, always somewhere an auction.

Seafood festivals abound, and regional food appears on every menu in infinite and delicious variation. The shorelines are filled with fishermen and women, boys with long poles and bare feet, crabbers with nets, and even some after the delicate frog legs in ponds, lakes, or swamps. Marshlands yield muskrats, a well known dish in these parts as are rabbit, squirrel, or venison served with sweet potato biscuits.

Its open farmland, left when the Ice Age moved in and out, has yielded some of the country's finest fruits and vegetables, and the popular firehouse dinners or church suppers always have bountiful helpings of seasonal asparagus, fresh-picked corn on the cob, peaches, oyster fritters, crab cakes, or southern cured hams. Old-fashioned amusements are close by at these events, so while you eat you can also watch serious horseshoe pitching, perhaps some pig rastling, or an auction, hear a band concert, or just visit on The Green.

Consult *The Philadelphia Inquirer* weekend listings or the Maryland Tourist Bureau. For routings call the Information Center at the Maryland House North ((301)287-2313), which is open from 9:00 a.m. to 5:00 p.m. weekdays, weekends, and holidays. Keep your maps handy.

Baltimore

There is something for every interest in this Eastern Shore region, and it is a short trip away into another world.

The major cities of Annapolis and Baltimore are in the fuller text. Below are only some of the other fascinating places you can easily find and enjoy! For more information call the Maryland Information Center ((301)490-2444), which is open from 8:30 a.m. to 6:00 p.m. Memorial Day to Labor Day. The rest of the year the hours are 9:00 a.m. to 5:00 p.m.

St. Michael's

James Michener lived here while writing his book *Chesapeake,* which tells much of the long history of the area. It is a picturesque little maritime town, home of the famous Baltimore clippers, the fastest ships of their day. Its indoor-outdoor museum on a large point is very well done. There is picnicking under the trees or you can gorge yourself at a wharfside restaurant. Wander in the town around St. Mary's

Square, which can give you some nice architecture. The museum offers a good local history (admission).

Easton

This gracious town has blocks of lovely architecture carefully restored and preserved by its citizens. Down on Washington Street beyond the hospital is the old Third Haven Meeting House, quietly set in a green park on the banks of the Tred Avon River. This is believed to be the oldest frame building dedicated to religious purposes in America. You are welcome to enter where William Penn preached with Lord Baltimore in the congregation or meeting. In the Village of Easton the Talbot Resolves were written before the Declaration of Independence, and the colonial Court of Justice was the first courthouse built in 1710.

Ask for a walking map at the Historical Society and see for yourself the old houses, some now used as offices. It has become a popular place to live, and you can easily see why. After stopping at the Historical Society, visit its shop across the street on South Washington Street, a fun place for browsing ((301)822-0773).

Oxford

This little town on the Tred Avon River has an interesting history and is a gem to see today. Here the rascally pirates Blackbeard and Stede Bonnet found refuge at Skillington's shipyards between Peachblossom and Trippe Creek. The wandering Arcadians on their long southward trek after being routed from their Nova Scotia homes by the British found refuge in Oxford in 1755. (Remember the poem *Evangeline*?) Once it was a port of entry and shipped tons of tobacco from nearby plantations, ship supplies, and produce from prosperous neighboring farms.

Today sailing regattas are popular, and Eastern Shore watermen still harvest clams, oysters, crabs, and fish from this harbor.

Stop at the Oxford Town Museum adjoining the Town Hall in the center of town, open to visitors without charge on Friday, Saturday, and Sunday from 2:00 p.m. to 5:00 p.m.. They will tell you more of Tench Tillman, who carried the news of Cornwallis's surrender at Yorktown; the old Acadamies; the Grapevine House; and how to ride the little Tred Avon Ferry that is run free, unattached to a cable! The Fishery Biological Research Laboratory is located in Oxford and is essential in helping the large national fishing industry of The Bay.

Trappe

About 13 miles from Easton is Trappe, the old town whose actual name has many clouded versions. Renowned John Dickinson lived here during his active years of the Revolution and the Continental Congress. His own handsome house is near Dover, Delaware, and is open to the public. Trappe Landing was once an important grain shipping point for barges and boats from Baltimore, but all that is only history now.

Fishing from the mile-and-a-half long bridge over the Choptank River brings many fishermen with tents for overnight sleeping (Route 50, 13 from Easton).

Talbot County, Maryland, has produced an excellent map and informative folder, which can be had for the asking. Write to The Talbot County Chamber of Commerce, Easton, Maryland 21606, or stop in while you are there.

Routing: This historic county is east of the Chesapeake Bay Bridge, following Route 301 and Route 50. Research your map for all these Bay towns.

Notes

Englishtown Auction and Flea Market

It is called the world's largest flea market and auction site, and it probably is! If you are an addict of either one, you will love it. If you have not already succumbed, you probably will after this adventure. It has been in existence since 1920 and growing every year in diversity. Open every Saturday from dawn (yes, dawn!) to 5:00 p.m., on Sunday it keeps more sedate hours of 9:00 a.m. to 5:00 p.m.. Seeing is believing!

Made for prowling or poking but mainly for serious buying, it brings regulars from five states who pour into the stalls of 200 merchants. First arrivals at early light are the knowing antique dealers from Connecticut, New York City, Lahaska, and the Delmarva Peninsula, all of whom can spot their prey from 50 yards. Outside tables resemble a mideastern bazaar with tides of people ebbing, flowing, and bargaining over unmatched shoes, clothing, groceries by the case, and patent medicines for every ache and pain known to man. Fortunes are told and horoscopes forecast. Celebrities from theatrical performances are always on the prowl for costumes or stage props. Coffins and antique cars find ready buyers, and once a real elephant was auctioned off to a cheering crowd.

Plan to spend a fascinating, unusual day, and when the gates clang shut, and the merchants pack up, drink your last cup of coffee, and hope that the parking lot for 8,000 cars will soon be cleared. Wear your sturdiest shoes, bring shopping bags if you want, and remember, "Let the buyer beware" is the only guarantee.

Routing: From Philadelphia cross into New Jersey and take the New Jersey Turnpike north to Exit 8. Take Route 33 east to Route 527. Go north to Englishtown and follow the large signs from the center of town.

Ephrata Cloister

Historic houses and buildings easily suggest the everyday life that once filled their rooms, but to step within the walls of Ephrata Cloister is an experience unlike any other in the country.

In the eighteenth century this village was the communal home of a radical German Protestant monastic settlement founded in 1732 by Conrad Beissel, a Pietist mystic. Under Penn's Holy Experiment, a tiny band of followers left their Rhenish countryside to carry their stringent way of life to the banks of the Cacalico River in Pennsylvania. Their strictly regulated community found purpose in constant service to God through severe self-denial and pious simplicity. Long hours of work, obedience, prayer, and one spare vegetarian meal a day demanded spiritual purification year round. All was under the eye and rule of Brother Beissel, who demanded that the celibate Brotherhood and Sisterhood live within tiny cells furnished with a board bed, a stone or wooden pillow, a narrow shelf, and a single candle. Some followers with families became so imbued that they left them behind to join the sect of the self-contained community.

Beissel and his followers clearly separated themselves from the Dunkards or Church of the Brethren to set up their own academy and meetinghouse, where they worhiped night and day. An occasional love feast was their only recreation, and one had to be particularly invited by the Orders to join this meager meal of thin lamb stew accompanied by much singing. Travelers always found a welcoming bed and board here without charge, and it was these devout and devoted people who cared for the sick and wounded after the disastrous Battle of Brandywine. Their little Mt. Zion Cemetery contains a monument to the hundreds who died while at the Cloister.

They developed many high skills in farming, milling, and carpentry and particularly in the arts of calligraphy and hand illumination of

Bible texts. Illuminated songbooks were filled with harmonious four- and six-part original hymns and can be seen in the Lecture Hall. Food preparation and endless domestic chores were completed in silence before they proceeded to assigned tasks of papermaking, printing on old German presses, and binding their high-quality books. The Sisters spent tedious hours beautifully writing and decorating the Frakturs, certificates of birth, marriages, or baptisms. These became a steady source of income, and many walked the 60 miles over rutted and snowy roads to Philadelphia and back to obtain or deliver orders.

The lush surrounding farms of the Amish and Mennonite country are quite a contrast; but once inside the split rail fences of the community, the sense of peace and tranquility is quite evident. Open fields, shade trees, lawns, and orchards surround the few buildings remaining, just as they were in the 1700s. The Lecture Hall has an informative film and exhibits with written materials to better help you understand this unusual sect. There is a conducted tour led by a guide in the white monastic robe worn by both Brothers and Sisters of the original community.

There are the large dormitory buildings where the sect slept and worked, and other large, wooden frame buildings are highly unusual as they are patterned after the medieval German architecture these people left behind. The separate dwelling used by Beissel himself is as austere in concept and furnishing as the rest.

You will bow low under arched doorways constructed to remind you of your humility, and see simple, old kitchen tools and unheated sleeping cells that were unlighted after dark, all faithfully maintained from the original days.

Houses nearby were built for spinning and weaving of linen and wool; printing presses; a mill; storage for the fruits of the orchards which are still standing and well tended; and a coolhouse for spring water.

To learn even more, attend the Vorspiel music drama at 9:00 p.m. on Saturdays and some Sundays in July and August. Weather permitting, performances are given in the amphitheater and, in case of rain, in the Saal on the grounds (admission). Space is limited so call (717)733-4811. There are pre-Vorspiel tours at 6:30 p.m. and 8:15 p.m.

Routing: Go west on the Schuylkill Expressway to the Pennsylvania Turnpike. Follow the Pennsylvania Turnpike west to Exit 21. Go south on Route 222 to Ephrata. The Cloister is found at the edge of Ephrata.

Notes

Fliers All!

The desire to fly,—to float on the back of the wind, has captured man's imagination since Icarus and his unfortunate experience with wings of wax. Was it only eighty short years ago that the indomitable Wright brothers raced across the sands of Kitty Hawk to "fly like a bird"?

A young child with his kite is also aloft with the eagles in his mind's eye.

Around Philadelphia, for those interested in various types of flight, there are many variations to the theme. For specific routes and times, check the Philadelphia Visitors Center at 15th and JFK Boulevard ((215)568-6599).

There are airports that offer flight training. Willow Grove Naval Air Station, just outside of Philadelphia, has a small, outdoor exhibit of older planes and some special event flying.

Gliding may be for those more free in spirit, and there is a lot of that around too. Professionals agree that from Allentown, Pennsylvania, southwest along the ridges of mountains into Maryland when the wind is right, there is not a better place to glide. "Best-kept secret in the U.S.A.," they laugh. "We join the birds in a new world!" Gliders are becoming more and more popular. "It's not that hard," says Dennis Pagan, noted glider pilot. "The birds sail right along with us, but in the spring, watch out for red-tailed hawks who don't want us near the little girl hawks in their territory!" In Blue Bell, Pennsylvania, you can take gliding lessons and flying lessons in small planes from 8:00 a.m. to 6:00 p.m. seven days a week. For gliders, there is usually a chase car as there is in ballooning, so you will find your way home again.

There is also a lot of ballooning. Benjamin Franklin sent the first "airmail" by balloon to New Jersey long, long ago, and people are still enchanted. Around Wilmington Airport in West Chester, Pennsylvania, they climb aboard at dawn to float in sheer rapture. Check it out ((215)696-9659). Near Lumberton, New Jersey, at the Burlington County Airport during the summer, there is one of the biggest airshows in the U.S.A. "If it flies, it will be here!" "Grab for the Gold" is their ballooning contest with alluring prizes such as a car or a motorcycle. All starts before 7:00 a.m., so be there early. Strasburg, Pennsylvania, has ballooning at their county fair with a prize race, skydiving, and helicopter rides. Ballooning starts at 6:30 a.m. (see Railroading text).

Flybys are popular too, with a great deal of precision flying and in good weather a parachute jump. For the earthbound watchers, there are displays of antique planes and cars, gliders, and experimental homemade crafts. Others are fascinated by the radio-controlled model planes. There is parking for 5,000 cars. A small admission fee is charged. The airport is at Mt. Laurel-Eayerstown Road southwest of Lumberton, New Jersey ((609)267-8207).

The newest sport, perhaps, is fun and games with the ultralights, small planes with lightweight motors. More than 20,000 devotees are up in the air with this fun, and an Experimental Aircraft Association with forty-eight chapters is in existence. Cessna Aircraft says they are outselling conventional light aircraft by three to one. The people at the Sweet Sky Shop in Doylestown, Pennsylvania, love to talk shop and can give you lots of information. Chatsworth, New Jersey, is also in the sales end of ultralights. If you want to be close to heaven, fly over the Pine Barrens early one morning to observe wild turkey and deer.

Perhaps you are a model plane fancier. New Jersey Sky Devils Club sponsors displays at Millville Airport, Cedarville Road, Millville, usually held on Sunday afternoons ((609)692-3178).

The Valley Forge Signal Seekers meet regularly every weekend in good weather from 9:00 a.m. to 5:00 p.m., from 9:00 a.m. to sundown on Saturday, and from 1:00 p.m. to sundown on Sunday at Valley Forge National Historical Park. Everybody is welcome! Turn left after entering the Park, and you will find the fliers close by and busy (see text).

These are sports and hobbies enjoyed by all ages, and everyone seems to like to share anecdotes and information; so if it is up in the air you like to be, there is lots of it in almost any form not far from Philadelphia.

Consult the Visitors Bureau for the sites of your choice.

Notes

The Franklin Mint Museum

The striking round museum building housing the exhibits of the Franklin Mint is the first expression of the uniqueness of this internationally known, privately operated collectors' haven which employs thousands of people. Set in the Brandywine countryside of Pennsylvania, it makes its own statement of excellence. Well-marked and providing good public parking on the grounds, it can be an interesting half-day visit that easily combines with either the nearby Battlefield or Brandywine River Museum at Chadds Ford (see text). It is also a good area for antiquing if that is your pleasure.

At the entrance to the museum is the famed Gilroy Robert's sundial, which tells time in the approved way but also gives the approximate day of the month and projects zodiacal constellation signs aligned with the sun and earth in this era. At the museum's door are the words of Thoreau, "It is the marriage of the soul with nature that gives birth to imagination." Soft music and tastefully lighted exhibits greet you directly inside. There is a beautiful shop to the left, and you will be enchanted with the small, slowly revolving carousel of enamel, gold, and porcelain in a gallery of exquisite treasures across the hall.

This private mint is a little more than twenty-five years old and has produced objects of silver, porcelain, pewter, china, leather-bound books, and collectors' furniture sent all over the world. Each series of beautiful objects from an individual artist's hands is commissioned by the Mint or by private orders and is available by subscription only. Once a series has been fully subscribed, it is never produced again.

Ask at the information desk for the next showing of the short film before you begin your wanderings through these absorbing galleries. They contain a complete World of Miniatures, including little English plates, kings and queens of England, porcelain bells banded in gold and decorated with alpine flowers, minicoins, a series of tiny English flower spoons, apostle spoons, and love spoons in the Welsh tradition.

The Franklin Mint revitalized the art of plate collecting for thousands of people who formerly could purchase only from Denmark and Britain. The ever popular American Currier and Ives plates are fashioned in pewter, while silver is used in the James Wyeth collector plates.

Graceful bronzes feature artists of the dance, and pewter sculptures show a series of Great American Cars and their hood ornaments.

Medals have long been popular with collectors and here you can see the unique fifty states Bicentennial collection of historic sites and cities.

There are also medallic jewelry, stamps of the world, and galleries with such titles as History of Aviation, Wild Life, Flowers and Brilliant Butterflies, Flags of All Nations, First-Day Covers, and State Spoons. There is also a Costeau collection. Thimbles are always attractive, and this collection uses well-known trademarks such as the Bon Ami chick or the Umbrella Girl of Morton's Salt.

There are also other special exhibits not located in the galleries mentioned above. Presidents of this country and abroad have selected porcelain sculpture as presentation gifts of state. You will see some that have been designed for Queen Elizabeth II, King Olaf of Norway, and Hirohito, among others. The Year of the Child, celebrated by the United Nations, has appealing figures designed by Carol Lawson, who also produced plates carrying familiar characters from Grimm's fairy tales. In addition to its constantly increasing Collector's Series, the Mint also accepts commissions for current coinage for various countries.

Once you could watch work in progress, but these days only the museum is open to the public, Tuesday through Saturday from 9:30 a.m. to 4:30 p.m. and from 1:00 to 4:30 p.m. on Sunday. It is closed on Monday and major holidays. There is no admission charge. For full information call (215)459-6168.

Routing: Go west on the Schuylkill Expressway and exit onto Route 1 (City Line Avenue). Follow Route 1 south to the museum, which is on the left after you pass Route 452.

Notes

Freedoms Foundation

Founded in 1949 as a nonpolitical organization to foster responsibilities of American citizenship in a contemporary world, this 105-acre campus lies appropriately adjacent to Valley Forge National Historical Park.

Its redbrick Colonial buildings include the Faith of Our Fathers Chapel, whose stained glass window is identical to that in the Prayer Room of the United States Capitol Building. There are others housing exhibits and records with appropriate names such as The Spirit of '76 Reading Room, The Patriots Hall of Fame, and the Key to Liberty exhibit listing the names of those who have received the Freedoms Foundation Award. There are also dioramas of Washington's grim days at Valley Forge. Recently a fascinating dioramoric interpretation of the various European explorations in this country has been added. The Knox Building, reached by walking across a wooden bridge, has a display of medals especially struck and donated by the Franklin Mint and also contains the only complete records in the United States of the heroes awarded the Medal of Honor, our country's highest honor for bravery.

A walking map can guide you through the 50-acre grove to the bronze statue of Washington at Prayer, Independence Garden marked with stones from the homes of each of the signers of the Declaration of Independence, and a 100-foot flagpole with its 24 $\times$ 42-foot flag that is illuminated at night. The grove is designed to give one acre to each of the states plus the District of Columbia and Puerto Rico. In each is an obelisk featuring the state seal and a plaque listing its Medal of Honor winners. Memorial trees and shrubs have been donated by individuals, groups, or clubs, and an Amvets memorial carillon rings the hours. Each Sunday in suitable weather the grounds are open to the hundreds of people who come to hear the band concert in the open-air amphitheater.

Their Distinguished Awards Program has honored more than 40,000 individuals, organizations, or corporations for untiring efforts to find better solutions to our social or human problems. Representatives from all walks of life have been honored, among them Bob Hope, Alistair Cooke, and Sandra Day O'Connor. In a special and moving ceremony at the White House, this award was accepted by the widow of Anwar Sadat. High school and accredited colleges receive awards for excellence in motivating their students to understand the role of private enterprise in the American way of life. Two dormitories house students who come together throughout the year for special seminars with nationally recognized leaders. The Foundation has forty-three volunteer chapters in twenty-one states who send students, give awards, seek out information, and disseminate the message of the Freedoms Foundation and its patriotic work.

An informative and inspirational visit to the Foundation could well be combined with a visit to Valley Forge National Historical Park nearby.

Visitors are welcome from 10:00 a.m. to 4:00 p.m. Monday through Friday, 10:00 a.m. to 4:00 p.m. Saturday, and 12:00 noon to 4:30 p.m. Sunday. Winter hours for all days from October through April are 10:00 a.m. to 4:00 p.m. There is no admission charge ((215)933-8824).

Routing: Go west on the Schuylkill Expressway to Route 202. Go south on Route 202 and follow signs to Valley Forge National Historical Park. Then follow Route 23 1 mile west of the Park.

Notes

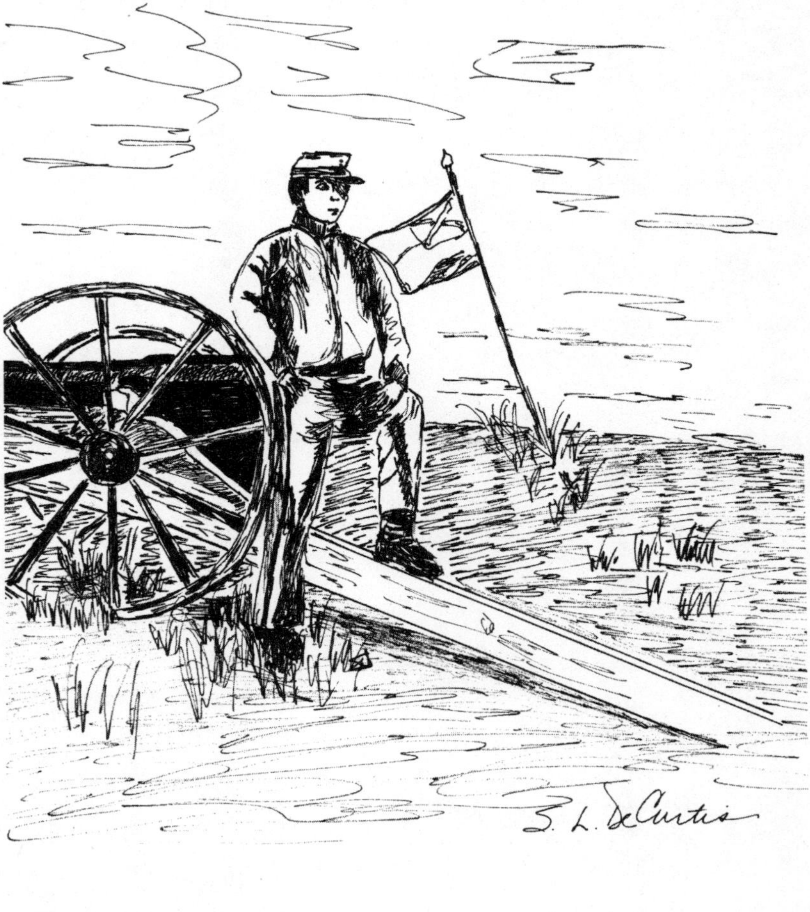
S. L. DeCurtis

Gettysburg

So many books and articles have been written by scholars and historians about the Battle of Gettysburg and the heroes of the bloody fields where this decisive battle was fought that no more can be added here. It is one of the nation's major military commemorative National Historical Parks and ranks in historic interest with Independence Park in Philadelphia and the various sites in Washington, D.C. It is the largest of the military battlefields with more than 1,000 monuments and many cannon along the 35 scenic miles you can travel in your own car. Battle sites are well marked, and you can get out to read markers or see the monuments at close range.

It is best to begin with the Information Center within the Park, where you will find designated parking (please observe), an informative film, and special information as to where a particular monument or statue you may be seeking is located. If you have time prior to your visit, you can write for full information.

The surrounding area is full of restaurants, motels, campgrounds, special museums, and various tours. These include an Auto-Tape-Tour, or a two-hour bus tour narrated by Raymond Massey, a Battle Orientation Electronic Map, and a wax museum. None of these are operated by the Park but may be just what you are looking for. A folder on the site will tell you where you can find all of them. All have various costs, of course.

Opposite the Gettysburg Park Visitors Center site is an enormous tower. This also is not run by the Park but offers a breathtaking view of the entire countryside and the battlefield. There is an elevator, and several levels have various attractions (admission).

In the town of Gettysburg one of the few original houses remaining open to the public was one commandeered by the Southern general,

Robert E. Lee, for his headquarters. There is no admission charge to enter and see many war relics.

Whatever your sentiments and your personal involvement with the Civil War, you will all want to stand where Lincoln stood as he mentally reviewed the short speech he had written to deliver at Gettysburg. For full information write to:

> GETTYSBURG TRAVEL COUNCIL
> DEPARTMENT 13 B
> 35 CARLISLE STREET
> GETTYSBURG, PENNSYLVANIA 17325
> (717)334-6274

The old town of Carlisle is not far away and also has some history to show. The Eisenhower farm ((717)334-1124) is also near and is open at certain hours during the week. Check at the Gettysburg Park Visitors Center. You are very close to both Lancaster and York, Pennsylvania, towns with much Colonial history and a glimpse of the Amish life-style in the beautiful farms that surround them (see text).

In Harrisburg (Pennsylvania's capital) is the William Penn Memorial Museum open Monday through Saturday from 9:00 a.m. to 5:00 p.m. and Sunday from 1:00 to 5:00 p.m. It is located directly north of the main capitol building at Third and North streets. Its four floors of exhibits could make a good combination with any of the sites near Gettysburg.

Routing: Go west on the Schuylkill Expressway to Route 202. Go south on Route 202 to the Route 30 exit. Proceed west on Route 30 to the Downingtown Bypass. Take the bypass and continue west on Route 30 directly to Gettysburg.

Notes

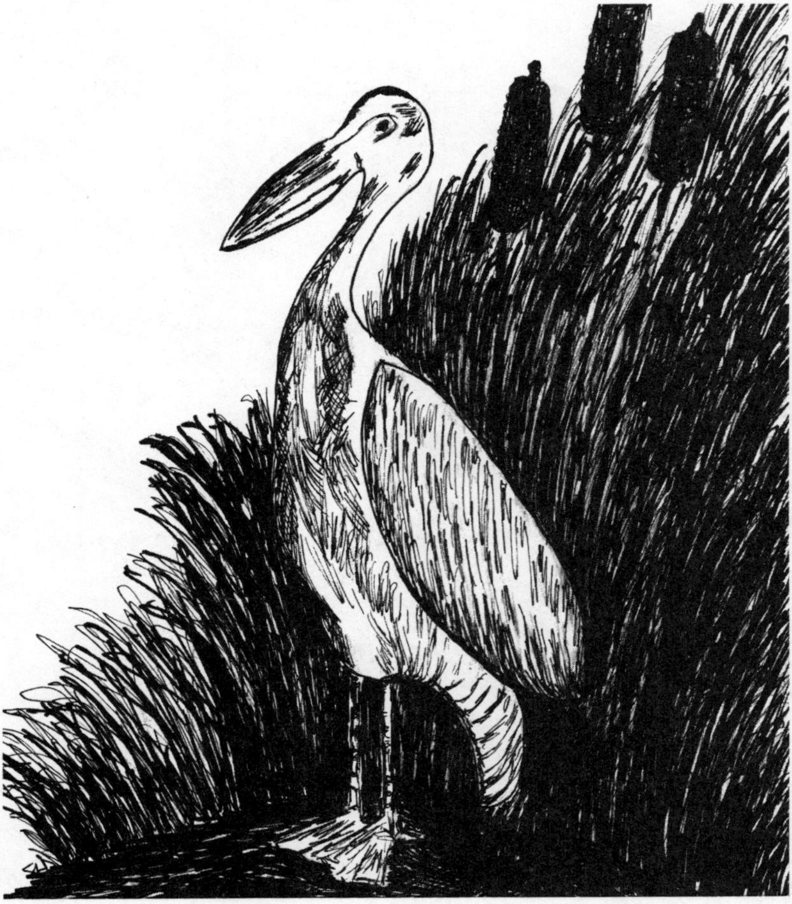

The Great Outdoors

Those with outdoor pleasure in mind can find something going on during four seasons of the year in Pennsylvania, New Jersey, Maryland, and Delaware.

All interests are served, whether it be active sports in the Pocono region of Pennsylvania, the long shoreline that edges New Jersey and Delaware, or the reaches of the great Chesapeake Bay of Maryland.

There are nature centers galore, Audubon Societies with programs, arboretums open to the public, special gardens with visiting hours, the great estate gardens of the many mansions, and, of course, Valley Forge National Historical Park just outside of Philadelphia (see text).

Check the weekend listings in *The Philadelphia Inquirer* for lots of information and phone numbers. Many places are suited to strolling, admiring, and picnicking. Others have marked nature trails with an available map at headquarters.

Some specialize in particular interests such as Bowman's Wildflower Preserve at Washington Crossing, Pennsylvania, or the great outdoor and indoor Longwood Gardens also in Pennsylvania. Many offer films or weekly events such as bog trots, night sky studies, or identification of edible wild foods.

There are great wildlife preserves such as Bombay Hook, Delaware, where thousands of wildfowl pass on the flyway or settle down in a natural surrounding. Brigantine, New Jersey, is also a favored place for migratory bird-watching. The Wetlands Institute in New Jersey has aquariums, exhibits, microscopes, observation towers, and salt marsh marked tours. Hawk Mountain in the Kittatinny Mountains of Pennsylvania is a private preserve with a breathtaking view, and in October it is the place to see hundreds of migrating eagles and hawks. At Sanctuary Headquarters there are exhibits and huge windows for viewing (admission).

For a listing of the many state parks with their lakes, waterfalls, creeks, trails, and special events, contact the Environmental Resources Department at the capital of each state. They can send you information. Specify if you want particular sites.

Large acreages of land are now being turned over to and cared for by conservancy societies or watershed associations, and many times they are open to the public for flower identification, canoeing, or walking. It is needless to remind you to be extra careful with cigarettes and matches in these cared for miles.

All these places can be reached from Philadelphia by car. Often you can bring your canoe or bike on the roof if that is how you want to spend your day. There is winter cross-country skiing in many places as well as downhill runs.

Peruse the text and contact the Philadelphia Visitors Center for addresses and phone numbers as well as folders that will also give you lodging or camping instructions.

Estate Gardens

The Pennsylvania Horticultural Society at 313 Third Street in Philadelphia ((215)625-8250) often knows of special garden tours or events. Longwood Gardens and Nemours Mansion in Pennsylvania are the grand gardens to visit (see The Brandywine Valley text).

Arboretums

The Morris Arboretum in Chestnut Hill, Pennsylvania, is open to the public (see text). The Tyler Arboretum near Media, Pennsylvania, is a beauty, and the Barnes Foundation (see text) in Gladwyne, Pennsylvania, also has rare species of trees, plants, and shrubs.

Nature Conservancies

The Brandywine Conservancy encompasses many hundreds of acres in a lovely valley setting with headquarters at the Brandywine Museum at Chadds Ford, Pennsylvania. There are nature trails, meadows, the stream itself, and local wild flowers well marked. You can buy packets of seeds in the museum gift shop. Also available for purchase is an unusual natural Christmas ornament of handmade "critters." These ornaments trimmed the White House Christmas tree in 1985.

Riverbend on Springmill Road, Gladwyne, has foot and horse trails through twenty-five acres of woods and open fields. There are frequent programs for the family throughout the year. It is open daily from 8:30 a.m. to sunset with no admission ((215)527-5234).

Watershed Associations

Pennypack Watershed has rambles along Pennypack Creek open to all with no admission. Call (215)671-0440 for information and directions.

Wissahickon Watershed at Four Mills Road in Ambler, Pennsylvania, has trails and a free museum. Call the Philadelphia Visitors Center ((215)636-3300) for a phone number.

Nature Centers

Schuylkill Valley Nature Center at 8480 Hagy's Mill Road (near Chestnut Hill, Pennsylvania) has 6 miles of trails through forest, ponds, and fields. Their museum and Discovery Room with multisensory exhibits is worth a visit. They have many special programs for all ages with low admission rates ((215)482-7300).

Churchville Nature Center, Churchville, Pennsylvania, has educational tours and programs of seasonal interest for all ages (no admission). Parents are invited to accompany children. There are also ten acres of a stream valley with ponds, fields, and wetlands. Its headquarters is located at Route 29 and Hollow Road in Phoenixville ((215)935-9777).

Mill Grove Center is the home where John James Audubon lived and worked as a young man. It has miles of wooded trails, feeding stations, nesting boxes and shrubs, and plants that invite the birds and bees. Call (215)666-5593 for hours (see text).

Wildlife Centers

Bombay Hook, Delaware, is the resting place for thousands of birds and marshlife. It is the happy winter home of hundreds of well-fed geese that fatten on dropped corn from nearby farms. Well-marked, it is near Dover, Delaware, in good open country.

Cape May Point beyond Cape May, New Jersey, has wetlands, a beach, and sandy trails for sea and marsh birds. Their headquarters has good exhibits.

Nature Preserves

Bowman's Hill Wild Flower Preserve, Washington Crossing, Pennsylvania, has trails, wild flowers, and a lookout tower.

Valley Forge National Historical Park is unique with much beautiful land left in its natural state. There are horse trails, walking, biking, and skiing trails. They have star watches, kite flying, and hillsides of pink-and-white dogwood trees in the spring that thousands from all over the nation journey to see. Aside from its historical interest, this immense park is a popular one year round ((215)782-7700).

Notes

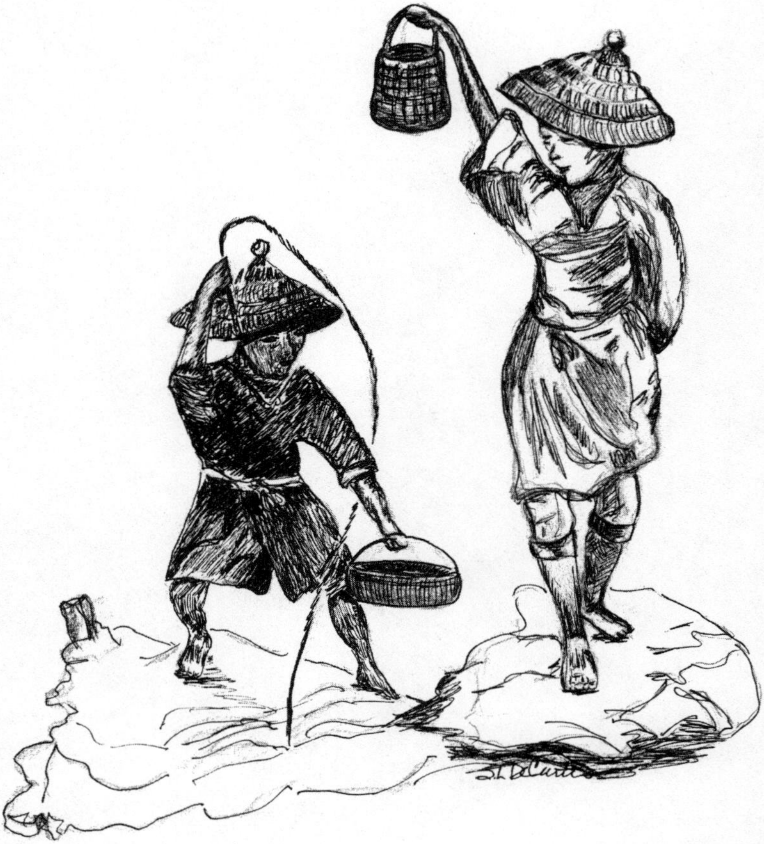

Green Hills Farm

Pearl S. Buck, internationally acclaimed author, was equally well known for her pioneer philanthropic work. Brought up in the Orient, daughter of Presbyterian missionaries, she spent many years in China at the turn of the century. She returned to graduate from Randolph-Macon College in Virginia, where she also taught psychology before rejoining her family. A few years later she married John Buck and with him moved to north China. While raising her own family, she also taught at the University of Nanking and later at Chung Yang University.

In 1925 she returned to this country to earn a master's degree at Cornell and began to write, submitting or retaining manuscripts based on her observations of the foreign country she had recently left. Her best-seller, of course, was *The Good Earth,* which was also made into a play and a movie. It won the Pulitzer Prize as the best novel of that year by an American and was soon translated into more than thirty languages. Books and articles began to pour out of the young, talented woman until she had finished her long trilogy, The House of Earth.

Following her subsequent marriage to Richard Walsh, president of the John Day Company, they set up housekeeping in 1935 in a comfortable stone farmhouse in the farmland of Bucks County. They adopted four children, and after his death she adopted five more, all of mixed Asian-American blood. Alarmed and saddened by the fate of these "new children," as she called them, she sought to bring attention to this new race of Amerasians, offspring of Orientals and American soldiers stationed in that part of the world. Unrecognized by their father, cast off by their mothers in desperation and disgrace in a country that abhorred both illegitimacy and mixed blood, the children were abandoned or left to run the streets as vagabonds.

In 1938 Pearl Buck was the first woman to receive the Nobel Prize for Literature awarded for her many books depicting genuine Chinese life. In 1948 she founded Welcome House, an adoption agency supported by her writings, that found homes for hundreds of the "new children." In 1964 the Pearl S. Buck Foundation won her the highest award of the government of the Republic of South Korea, and once again she expanded her tireless efforts at this philanthropy. She died at eighty-one, beloved and honored worldwide, and at her own request is buried at Green Hills Farm facing, in the Chinese custom, the rising sun.

Her house is just as she left it with the addition of a gallery built to show her honors, awards, and degrees. You will see her writing table in the living room, the many Oriental furnishings throughout the house, her Chinese gowns hanging in her closet, and a beautiful display of Oriental objects in a special case. She built a writing wing with a comfortable living room containing a large fireplace. Pieces of her own sculpture sit where she placed them, and the greenhouse where she and her husband pursued their hobby of raising camellias still shows profuse blooms each January.

There are many seasonal events at Green Hills Farm, so you may want to call ahead ((215)242-6779). There are guided tours throughout the house and grounds daily at 10:00 a.m. and 2:00 p.m. Monday through Friday, except legal holidays (admission).

You are not far from Fonthill or the Moravian Tile Museum, part of the Mercer Mile (see text) near Doylestown for a combination day.

Routing: Go north on Broad Street to Route 611. Continue north on Route 611. Take the bypass through Chalfont. Go left on Route 313 and follow to Dublin. Turn left on Maple Avenue, which becomes Dublin Road. You will see signs for Green Hills Farm. Ample parking is available on the grounds.

Notes

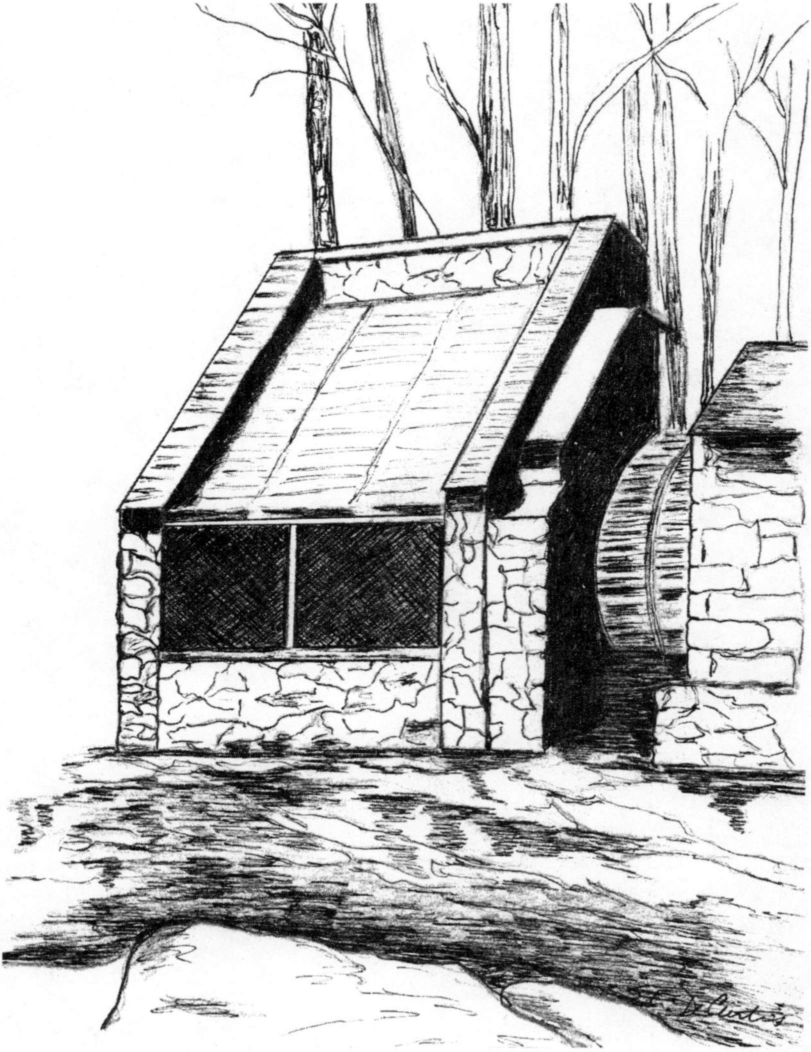

Hagley Museum and Mills

One of the most unique indoor-outdoor museums is the interesting large site of the old Hagley mills, the largest black powder mills in America.

Originally a gristmill for grinding local grains plus a sawmill, its sixty-two acres were purchased by E. I. Du Pont de Nemours to produce much needed gunpowder before the Revolution. The yards also supplied powder for the War of 1812, the Civil War, and World War I when obsolescence closed this skillful and dangerous work. However, blasting powder was much in demand for the constant building of roads, tunnels, and bridges as urbanization spread. Blasting powder was another large area of production for the nation, particularly in this region. Today the Du Pont Company is widely diversified in many fields of research and production, but this industry site of the past is carefully maintained.

The large French chateau residence is also maintained with its charming eighteenth-century garden. The entire former village is for walking, and there is an excellent tour map to use. Stop first at the main museum building with its "talking map." Then start out on your own to see the Rolling Mills, the Engine House, the First Office, the Cooper Shop, and more than a dozen others. In the original Machine Shop is the Black Powder Exhibit to explain the entire black powder process. It is also the theater for a short film and a list of buildings where daily demonstrations take place. The area is a pleasant one along the banks of the Brandywine River so you may take a picnic. There are tables, restrooms, and an excellent museum shop. The Eleutherian Mills Residence stands on a rise apart from the gunpowder plant and has a formal French garden in the European style. A short distance away are the First Office and Du Pont's Experimental Workshop. The Steam House contains a restored engine and boiler, and there is a narrow gauge railroad partially restored. There is also a stone quarry where granite was quarried to construct the many buildings. The site, now 200 acres large, is dedicated to the preservation and the interpretation of one of the country's old heritages.

It is open Tuesday through Saturday and holidays from 9:30 a.m. to 4:30 p.m. On Sunday it is open from 15:00 p.m. It is closed Monday, Thanksgiving, and New Year's Day. For information write to the Hagley Museum, Greenville, Delaware 19807 or call (302)658-2401.

Routing: Take I-95 south. Exit at Route 202. Go north to Route 141 and turn left to the museum complex which is well marked.

Notes

Harpers Ferry

This once violent but now peaceful spot lies at the confluence of the Shenandoah and Potomac Rivers in the Blue Ridge Mountains of West Virginia. Here in the early 1700s Peter Stephens tied his canoe and marked it an excellent place for a ferry on the North-South Indian Trail. By 1733 water and overland traffic increased, proving him correct. Later Robert Harper managed the ferry as the village grew large enough to support a gristmill. By 1800 it was a thriving community, including several offshore islands.

Following the Revolution, Washington remembered the site from his young surveying days and appealed to Congress to designate it a national arsenal. They saw the advantage of its easily defensible position and soon built an arsenal and a house for its master armourer in charge.

By 1825 the town boasted an inn and tavern, a blacksmith's shop and small forge, a dry goods store, and many citizens fully employed at the Arsenal. A pharmacy and a confectionary shop opened and were well used during weekly market days.

On Virginius Island in the Shenandoah River stood Hall's Rifle Works, which made excellent breech-loading rifles with the new concept of interchangeable parts that set the path for eventual mass production of this firearm.

Harpers Ferry brings to mind the flamboyant raid of John Brown, a fanatical man burning to liberate slaves and found a safe town for their refuge. Bolstered by articles and funds from New England liberals, he planned a raid on the Arsenal in 1859. With only twenty-two men but guns blazing, he seized a few key points in a surprise attack. Local militia were called and Brown was captured, tried, and hung for treason, murder, conspiracy, and insurrection against the federal government. At the start of the Civil War the Union quickly removed arms stored in the town, and the Armoury was razed against seizure by the Confederates. Before the nearby Battle of Antietam, Stonewall Jackson captured 12,700 Union troops billeted here. Following the war, the townspeople, exhausted and unemployed, moved farther west; and final devastation came with torrential floods that swept the town, demolishing many buildings. By 1900 Harpers Ferry lay almost obliterated from the map.

Reclaimed today by the National Park System, it is waiting for you to walk the streets, enter restored buildings, and visit the information headquarters in the old inn. A visit to the master armourer's house will show you the story of gun-making in this country. Many foundations of former village buildings are being excavated, and the old firehouse stands to show you what a small refuge it became for a man with such large ideas! Walk up the hill through the new town and visit the excellent bookstore and the church set high on the ridge at the top of the stone steps. For full information, call the Visitors Center ((304)535-2482). The town is open year round with special events during the good weather. There is good picnicking nearby, hiking on marked trails, and the old C&O Canal Towpath. Camping information and registration for mountain climbing is a must at the Ranger Station.

You may want to continue on to Antietam (Sharpsburg) Battlefield nearby. Check with park staff at Harpers Ferry. You are also not far from Washington, D.C., or Baltimore, Maryland (see text).

Routing: Go south on Broad Street to I-95. Go south on I-95 to Route 695 and proceed west to I-70. Go west on I-70 to U.S. 340 and go south. You will see signs to Harpers Ferry.

Notes

Historic Fallsington

The delight of this charming village is that it exists at all! This historic market town on the banks of the Delaware River in Bucks County, Pennsylvania, has retained its quiet existence even through three centuries, serene in its reflection of former times.

In 1690 a Quaker meetinghouse was built to accommodate this growing congregation, who welcomed their neighbor, William Penn, who lived 5 miles away at Pennsbury Manor (see text). There is an old log house, the Moon-Williamson House, which was built around 1685 and is noted as being the oldest house in the state standing on its original site. Swedish and English architecture are both reflected in its varied styles. Two enormous sycamore trees here are believed to have been planted by Samuel Moon in 1767. The village center is Meeting House Square with not one but three houses of worship! An old stone house, believed to have been a tavern in 1798, was at subsequent times a post office, a jail, a library, a fraternal lodge, and a store. The Gambrel Roof House near the Square has an original section dated 1728 and was also a meetinghouse at one time. During the nineteenth century it was a girls' boarding school, later a library, and then a day school. In 1788 John Merrick, a cordwainer, built what is now known as the Pleasants' House with its date marked high on the gable. A heart is also carved in the pent roof to the north. Inside an original walk-in fireplace and a stone sink remain. The Burges-Lippincott House is known for its beautiful doorway and is believed to have been built before the Revolution. It was owned in the early 1800s by Joseph Kelly, a carpenter, and it is thought that it was he who added the interior woodwork and door.

In the Victorian days the population grew slowly, enlivened by young ladies from the city who were brought to better circumstances in this little country town. With a population of 340, Fallsington had a blacksmith shop, a post office, three shoemakers, a tinsmith, a paint shop, two doctors, and an inn.

At the conclusion of World War I, the proprietress of the tavern gave a welcome home party for returned Fallsington "boys" and had their pictures taken with herself in her Red Cross uniform!

Stop at the old store for a walking map or to join a guided tour (admission), Wednesday through Sunday from 11:00 a.m. to 4:00 p.m., from November 15 to March 15. You will see an audiovisual presentation, visit several houses plus the Schoolmaster's House at the edge of town. There are several lovely houses up the hill from the old square and a pleasant library with a handsome pair of carriage lamps at the door.

A visit to nearby Pennsbury or the town of New Hope makes a good combination for this day in the country.

For special events, days, and tour times, call (215)295-6567.

Routing: Take I-95 north. Exit at U.S. 1. Go north on U.S. 1, then left on Tyburn Road.

Notes

Hope Lodge

This handsome 200-year-old house was built for the prosperous Quaker miller, Samuel Morris. Empty and doomed to destruction, it was purchased in 1922 by William Degn who, after restoring and furnishing it, gave it to the care of the Pennsylvania Historical and Museum Commission. It stands in open fields surrounded by a barn, an orchard, and a bricked terrace overhung with grapevines.

In true Quaker style, the unknown architect-builder used only the best materials for the house. The woodwork is of special interest in the pilasters by doorways, moldings, panelings, and pediments. The windowsills are wide and deep, showing the thickness of the outer walls both for temperature control and safety.

The bright blue shade of the painted woodwork may surprise some visitors from other parts of the country, but local ones will recognize the same colors used at the Peter Wentz Farmstead and others in the Dutch country.

A very wide, high-ceilinged center hall runs the width of the house with large doors opening to the outside at each end. One is the handsome Georgian-style front entrance with a small overhanging eave, and the other leads to a Georgian green boxwood garden. Halls in many houses of this period were used for more than passageways to other rooms. They often served as informal rooms in themselves for teatime, small groups of visitors, instruction of servants by the master of the household, or, on some occasions, for dancing parties following suppers or dinners.

The old summer kitchen is low-beamed and is furnished with a country trestle table, a deacon's bench, and slat-back chairs. Herbs hang from the rafters, and the door of the bake oven is open as though ready to receive the long loaves of bread.

The formal dining room has a set of shield-back chairs and blue-banded china carrying the crest of the West family who later owned the house. An even later owner gave the property its name of Hope Lodge in thanks to his uncle, whose family was of Hope Diamond fame.

Morris himself was a genial bachelor said to be deeply in love with a lady who did not return his affection, but the beauty of his home and the ample style in which he planned large meals for many guests give a hint of his popularity.

Bedrooms upstairs are well furnished with the master bedroom overlooking the area where the mill once stood. A second room is done in a later style with bright wallpaper and shuttered windows.

The third floor, once used to house servants and slaves, was commandeered for hospital use during the Revolutionary War.

The cellar compartments show a large winter kitchen with a dumbwaiter rising to the dining room above and several storage rooms, one with a trough where a stream flowed through keeping milk, fruits, eggs, and other perishables at a cool temperature. The original large hooks for fowl, game, meats, and smoked provisions are imbedded in the ceiling beams.

Hope Lodge is open Tuesday through Saturday, 9:00 a.m. to 5:00 p.m., year round and on Sunday from 12 noon to 5:00 p.m. Admission is required. For more information call ((215)646-1595).

Routing: Go west on the Schuylkill Expressway to Route 1 (City Line Avenue). Follow Route 1 north to Route 611. Take Route 611 north to Ogontz Avenue (Route 309) and turn left. Take Ogontz Avenue to Route 73 and turn left. Follow to Whitemarsh and the house.

Notes

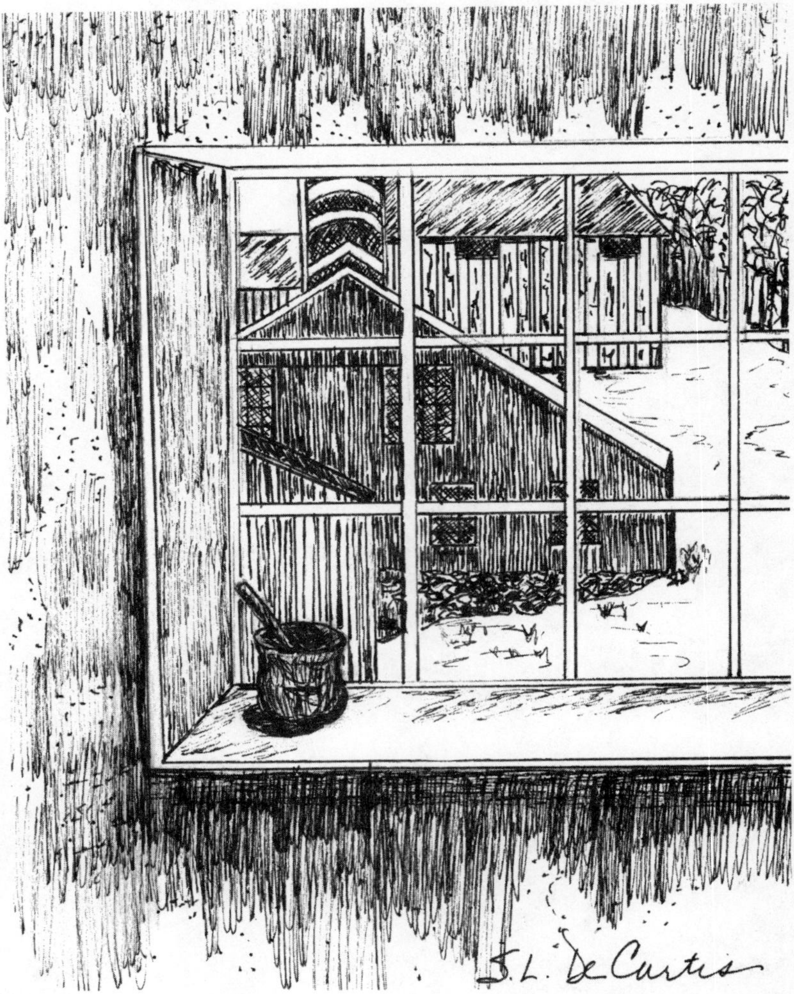
S.L. DeCurtis

Hopewell Village

This entire village restoration of seventeen sites is a National Historic Designation of Pennsylvania and lies near Birdsboro at the end of the Lenape Indian trail of early years.

In 1750 England decreed the Iron Act, forbidding Colonials to make iron products. Raw materials were to be shipped in English vessels back to the mother country, there fashioned into saleable goods, then shipped once more to the colonies for their consumption. This law was weakly enforced and, in most cases, ignored.

Clement Brooke, ironmaster of Hopewell Furnace, looked at this new decree of the Crown with scant interest. His little village of Hopewell was thriving, produced iron, had a fine supply of woodland for charcoal needed in the furnaces, contained content and fully employed inhabitants, and had a market for his high quality iron.

Hopewell Furnace and its surrounding working buildings and dwellings were built by French Creek in 1771 and turned out pig iron to be sent to nearby forges for tools, wagon fittings, hinges, locks, bolts, firebacks, and many other minor necessities. Pay was carefully scaled by the paymaster. The village clerk ranked highest in the scale, for he wielded the power of cash and chits at the company store. He was also charged with overseeing the constant flow of essential limestone, charcoal, and raw iron.

Wives and daughters tended to their own homes with food preparation, spinning, weaving, baking, and sewing. Jobs were also available in the little village or at the Manor House, where living was on a higher and more elegant style. Cooks, maids, nurses, grooms, and drivers were needed for the running of that household, which saw a frequent flow of guests from Philadelphia, Baltimore, New York, and smaller towns in between. Visits from afar were long ones, and entertainment was happily provided year round. Holidays, election days, Military Musters, country balls, and dinners were weekly affairs when guests brought news and gossip, as well as opportunities for fun or romance.

Mark Bird, who built Hopewell Furnace, played an important part in Revolutionary history of the area as a member of the Committee of Correspondence, a colonel in the county militia, and deputy quartermaster general to Washington's troops at Valley Forge. He later became a member of the Pennsylvania Assembly and a Berks County judge. Losing several furnace properties after the Revolution, he died impoverished in 1814 in North Carolina.

By the mid 1830s the shadow of obsolescence hung over Hopewell as the "black diamond," coal, replaced charcoal. Transportation was becoming more expensive, and larger furnaces were built using newer methods. One by one the little, independent furnaces "blew out," leaving cold hearths. By 1900 they had disappeared.

At Hopewell Village you may enter the Manor House and the little surrounding cottages. There are a spring house, a country barn with its wagons and stables, an old blacksmith's shop, and other sites that give a good picture of self-sufficient life.

Hopewell Village is open daily except Christmas and New Year's Day. During the summer months there are many activities demonstrating the trades and crafts of former times. There are also picnicking and camping on assigned sites nearby in French Creek State Park ((215)582-8773).

Routing: Go west on the Schuylkill Expressway to the Pennsylvania Turnpike. Follow the Pennsylvania Turnpike west to the Morgantown Interchange. Take Route 23 east and Pennsylvania 345 north.

Notes

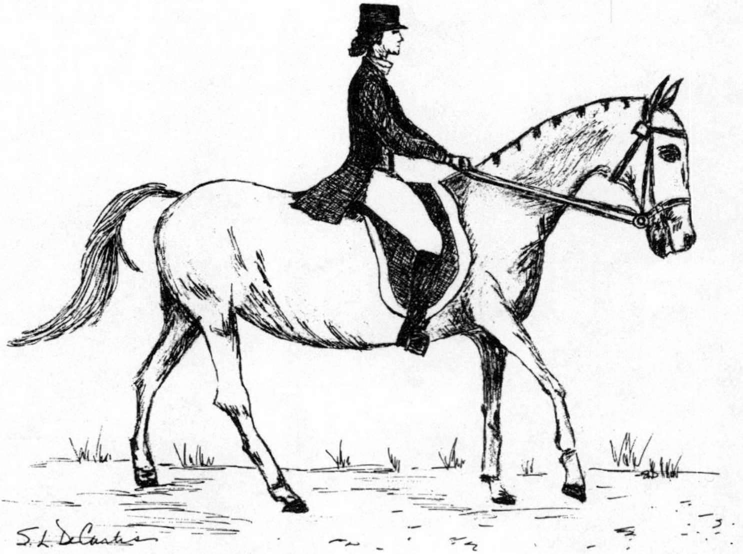

Horses

You may think Virginia, Florida, and the Wild West are the home of the horse. You are right, of course, but around Philadelphia you will find the largest horse show in the United States, superb equine competitions, countryside steeplechase, fox-and-hound rides in the rolling countryside, the elegant art of dressage, precision riding, pony shows, horse auctions and sales, and lively rodeos. Whether you are a knowledgeable participant or an enthusiastic spectator, you can find something to please year round.

Horses, fine breeds and farm animals, are on sale most weekends somewhere in Chester or Lancaster counties. Check the sale pages of *The Philadelphia Inquirer* for locations. There are also shops galore for riding habits, tack, saddles, boots, or whatever you may require in custom clothes or equipment. Many of the Main Line, Chester County, and Chestnut Hill galleries also have good hunting prints for a collection, so browsing in those areas will be fun.

The Sunday parades at the Valley Forge Military Academy in Wayne, Pennsylvania, have excellent mounted riders, and in the month of May the Grand Prix Olympic Style Jumping Contest attracts people from the entire country. It's an exciting occasion. Call the Academy at (215)688-1800 for time and date.

In June the annual Devon Horse Show is a benefit event that has been held for eighty-seven years, and to come away with a Devon Blue is heaven for the greats of the equestrian world. It is also a week-long series of social brunches, lunches, teas, dinners, and midnight suppers in Main Line homes and clubs. Or it can be just plain fun for everyone at the stalls, gourmet shops, little eateries, and people-watching. Preparation for this enormous ten-day event is year round for the industrious committees as 150,000 people come to this, the country's largest outdoor show, on the Devon Fair Grounds. There are barns, bleachers, and very limited parking, so we advise taking the Paoli Local train from Suburban Station and getting off at Devon and crossing Lancaster Pike. You will see the long blue buildings and cannot possibly lose your way.

The show was started in 1896 as a spring outing for the gentry, who liked to compare their horses and carriages and bonhomie. In 1929 their ladies began serving tea from their own silver teapots and turned the fun to beneficial purposes. A local hospital has received more than four million dollars from this event.

There are all kinds of special events such as a local carriage parade, sometimes a special mounted police show, or the crack equestrian team from the Valley Forge Military Academy down the road. There is an evening Grand Prix for jumping and many popular junior events, including the Great Falls Pony Club's vaulting team of bareback devilry. But the main events are horses and riders in the Dixon Oval, where you will see the international finest. You shouldn't miss this event whether you are a rider, a horse breeder, or a lover of horse shows and the special skills of exhibition. It is a truly wonderful week and deserves its national fame.

In September the Devon Horse Show Grounds hosts for one week the annual Gold Cup Grand Prix, which attracts people with a special interest in jumping. Beautifully trained mounts compete in clearing hurdles that start at 5 feet and include combinations of water and fences that the horse must clear, leaving his rider high and really dry. This is a high-caliber sport of Olympic quality, and there are scouts as well as well-wishers in the large attendance. Again, take the Paoli Local train from Penn Center Station and get off at Devon. There is a gate admission ((215)951-8879).

The three-day Radnor Hunt is another hospital benefit farther along the Pike. This 100-year-old Chester County Hunt draws national championship contestants who measure their own speed, strength, and skill on fine mounts with extraordinary endurance. Under fall skies, rain or shine, hardy spectators enjoy gourmet picnics while visiting with houseguests and friends as they watch these cross-country races. School figures are featured with dressage on Thursday and Friday, and the highlight of the hunt is on Saturday with horse and rider covering 18 miles of countryside jumping fences, hedges, and streams. Now and then there is a fallen rider or two. There are bleachers, a big tent with wonderful foods and drink, and an overall casual air both in the grandstand and around the grounds. The hunt is held on Providence Road, which you can find in Chester County near Malvern. It is north of Route 3 in Willistown Township. For information call (215)388-7601.

The annual Winterthur Point-to-Point recreates a very old interest in horse racing with wonderful silks worn by some of the best jockeys in the world. Held in the countryside surrounding the beautiful Winterthur Museum and Gardens, it is a popular fund-raiser for this mansion, which was the home of Henry Francis Du Pont in Delaware. Silver racing trophies have been coveted since Colonial days in this area and still are.

There is something for everybody here, too, with top price patrons, seats that feature lunch in horse-drawn carriages, private admission to the Winterthur Museum and Gardens, and a special reception following the race in the Garden Pavilion. There is, of course, a general admission, which admits you to picnic and parade with the country's wealthiest racing enthusiasts who will spring to their feet and scream just as enthusiastically as you when that bell sounds and the horses start. This is one of the area's most colorful events, and a visit to the Winterthur Museum is not to be missed (see text). It is truly one of the great houses of America. The atmosphere of the day completely matches the grandeur of the site.

Take Interstate 95 south to Route 52 north, exit in Wilmington, and follow the road 5½ miles north to the Winterthur entrance on the right. Phone first for Point-to-Point specific information ((302)654-1548).

In Shartlesville, Pennsylvania, the heart of the Pennsylvania Dutch country, usually in June, there is a registered Appaloosa Show. There are also lots of rodeos and horse shows scheduled throughout the entire summer. These are held at Mountain Springs Camping Resort near Reading, so leave your silk dresses and big hats at home. This is a family camping ground on a 100-acre farm with swimming, hayrides, fishing, a playground, and good hiking on the nearby Appalachian Trail or marked nature trails. There is lots to see and do in addition to the rodeos. There are hookups, restrooms, shower facilities, a laundromat, camp store, phone, church services—almost anything to give a family a relaxed stay whether you have your van or pitch a tent.

For those who want more exploring when they tire of horses, you will find that there is much historic interest as well as lots of discount shopping in nearby Lancaster and York (see texts).

You can write Mt. Springs Camping Resort at P.O. Box 365, Shartlesville, Pennsylvania 19554 ((215)488-6859). They have a printed program of events.

Routing: One mile north of Shartlesville, exit off Route 22 (Interstate Route 78).

There is also good trail riding in the Pennsylvania Dutch country. In Lititz, Pennsylvania, in the rich, rolling hills and farmlands (follow your map), Maggie Price has initiated trail riding competitions. She knows that there are many not interested in the social aspects of horse shows and with growing success has run the Cornwall Competitive Trail Ride for several years. This sport began in Vermont a few years ago, and now riders come here from five states with their vans, horses, and friends. There are now more than 500 members of the Eastern Competitive Trail Riding Association, whose riders must pace their horses over a set course in a given time. In this sport, time is controlled rather than beaten and a team is penalized for coming in either too early or too late! They must survive and arrive at the goal in good condition within the four to four-and-a-half-hours of the 25-mile ride. Winners are selected by a point system plus the judges' notes.

At the present time, the sport attracts more women than men. The women claim that they have more patience and tact to succeed. You will see gorgeous Appaloosa and Arabian breeds here and riding gear that is comfortable and not found in the fashionable pages. One year's winner wore her "best" jeans and boots well covered with Cornwall mud well suited to the great outdoors of Lebanon County.

If it's a day's riding you want without competition, there are bridle paths and trails in the Chestnut Hill area of Wissahickon Creek in Fairmount Park. Call the Philadelphia Recreation Department ((215)686-2176) for horse information and directions as well as the strictly observed regulations.

One of the best riding areas is at Bellevue State Park, Delaware. The mansion of William Du Pont offers the finest of equestrian programs complete with stables, an indoor track, outdoor trails, and professional instructors. You will find it just off I-95 and the Marsh Road exit.

Ridley Creek State Park also has facilities on a 4-mile trail through the woods, fields, and beside a stream. Call the Keen Stables (215)566-0942) in Media, Pennsylvania, for directions and fees.

The Sheeder Mill Farm in Spring City, Pennsylvania, offers trail lessons on its 50 miles for riding. You will be tested before you leave the stable as to the right size of your mount with instructions of how to mount and a demonstration of your abilities to ride on a half-mile track behind the stable. This is a very good idea before you start off with your guide at a cost of less than ten dollars an hour. There are also overnight trail rides that can be arranged, which include overnight camping on a small island in the center of a pond or by a creek. It's lots of fun for those who like to cook out or fish.

No need for riding habits, but do wear long pants or jeans, no halters as you could get scratched by low tree branches, and it's a good idea to bring a sweater or a jacket. It can rain even on a pretty summer day. (Use your Pennsylvania map for routing).

As you can see, horses are a part of Pennsylvania life in many ways. You may need a car to go to some of these sites, but a day with horses can give you a special type of fun and excitement whether you watch or ride!

Contact the Philadelphia Visitors Center for phone numbers and more complete information.

Notes

A Journey on the Great Germantown Road

Historians agree that Germantown is unique.
They also are still having gentle disagreements on the nationality of its first settlers! Were they Germans or Dutch? There seems to be evidence of both, and we have to remember that the people of Lancaster County to whom we refer as Pennsylvania Dutch are actually of German descent. But perhaps with the birth of the Dutch Republic in the 1600s and its haven of welcome to all nations, this confusion in terms is understandable.

This new government bade a political farewell to its former ties with Spain and its powerful Roman Catholic Church. The tiny country of Holland embraced refugees, freethinkers, and actual dissidents in a wholesome, hearty way. Its trade was flourishing worldwide, its merchant fleet making burghers rich, and its new art flourishing as never before.

Many European eyes were turning firmly westward to America, and enticing real estate offers were advertised daily to persons willing to sail and settle in the New World.

Germantown, Pennsylvania, was founded in 1683 by the foresighted Francis Daniel Pastorius, a Quaker lawyer for the Frankfort Corporation, which had purchased from William Penn 15,000 acres of land. He had clearly in mind establishing a town quite separate from nearby Philadelphia. It was to be a trading and manufacturing town, he decided, for the soil could not compete with the farmlands of western Lancaster or easily accessible New Jersey. It should thus supply fresh produce from small market gardens, have workshops for both crafts and tradesmen, and provide convenient warehouses for storage of goods en route to Philadelphia that lay only 5 miles to the south.

The Great Road (later Germantown Road) early on was a muddy dirt track often mired in rain or snow. This only proved to be an incentive to the manufacture of wagons especially designed for such a rough passage. Its many creeks had good, fresh water and became the sites for gristmills or paper mills along the Wissahickon or the deeper Schuylkill.

Germantown soon attracted a continuous influx of emigrating Huguenots, Irish, Swedes, Blacks, and English, who set up housekeeping quite happily in this thriving community.

In 1730 a brick kiln was erected but soon gave way to the more thrifty use of fieldstone for houses set neatly in rows next to the street. No English pocket flower gardens here! Only grander mansions stood in open grounds with their formal gardens, orchards, and outbuildings to the back.

There was plenty of good water, advertisements reveal, which also attracted tanners, weavers and dyers, carpenters, masons, and cordwainers. The first paper mill in America was established here by William Rittenhouse in 1690 and was well known throughout the early colonies for its excellent products.

Religious freedom followed quite naturally with Quakers, Mennonites, Moravians, Dunkards, German Reformed, and Lutheran congregations finding hospitable spiritual homes. In 1688 a group of Germantown citizens signed a petition protesting slavery, which was sent to the Yearly Meeting of Friends.

The energetic little community enjoyed continued prosperity until 1777 when the Great Road was filled with the red-coated British army under the command of General William Howe, who was occupying Philadelphia. Soldiers were billeted in almost every home with larger houses commandeered for officers in charge.

On October 4 of that year Washington made a courageous attack on Germantown from nearby Valley Forge but was forced to an orderly retreat. All was not lost, however, for this was one incident that persuaded the French to come to the aid of the struggling Revolutionary Army and the battle was hailed abroad as a diplomatic success.

In 1793 and 1794 a disastrous yellow fever epidemic ravaged Philadelphia, literally wiping out hundreds of its citizens in a very short time. Those who could fled to Germantown on the Great Road to find residence where "the airs and waters are more healthful."

Many so enjoyed the new country life with its proximity to sophisticated Philadelphia that they became permanent residents. They expanded the service trades, cobbled the streets, and filled the schools and churches. Little Germantown had become a sought-after suburb!

The Great Road was widened to accommodate a scheduled coach route and a daily procession of carriages, and with the advent of the railroad in the 1800s textile mills sprang up almost overnight.

This spine of transportation now needed access roads, so streets running north and south were built, which soon accommodated more commuters in nearby Mt. Airy and Chestnut Hill.

Each spring there is now an annual tour sponsored by the Germantown Historical Society when historic sites along the Great Road can be visited. There are as many as twenty-three sites at your convenience.

Doors are open wide with traditional hospitality, there are guides to interpret, fresh flowers bloom indoors and out, and in some places you can browse among books or buy fresh herbs from a choice selected stock.

Flat-heeled shoes are a must, not only for comfort but also to preserve the beautiful old floors and rugs. There is good parking on the side streets and convenient lots.

Tickets and information for Tour Day can be purchased at the Historical Society, 5214 Germantown Avenue ((215)848-0514). Fees are nominal.

Of course, you can visit year round, for many of these historic houses, schools, and churches are open during their own designated hours. These vary, so contact the Historical Society by phone ((215)324-2877) before you set out. They have brochures and a walking map.

You will be rewarded by periods of history that reflect the early Colonial days, perilous Revolutionary times, Federal development in splendid mansions, and the later romantic Victorian gingerbread-style villas. Take a camera and walk the side streets as well and you will see a wealth of architecture varied enough to please many tastes.

Germantown on the Great Road will give you a day to remember!

GERMANTOWN HISTORICAL SOCIETY
   MUSEUM COMPLEX
5214 GERMANTOWN AVENUE
((215)324-2877)

This is the place to start. The Visitors' Orientation Center is in a fine Federal house built in 1796. There is also a good museum of American decorative arts here. In the Baynton House are a library and local archives of Germantown and area history. The Howell House, a stone companion to the brick Baynton House, was also built by William

Forbes and has a lovely museum of dolls, toys, and quilts. The modern building known as the Von Trott Museum Annex has good displays of agricultural and domestic tools and implements that will interest the gentlemen of your party while the ladies enthuse over the Howell House exhibits. The Bechtel House was the home of Johannes Bechtel, built in 1742 for this stalwart leader of the German Reformed and Moravian churches. Historic costumes and period dress are shown in the Clarkson-Watson House. This entire complex is open (with some variation) on Tuesday and Thursday, from 10:00 a.m. to 4:00 p.m. and on Sunday from 1:00 to 5:00 p.m. (admission).

WYCK
6026 GERMANTOWN AVENUE,
GERMANTOWN, PA
((215)-848-1690)

This interesting house is one of the oldest in the entire Philadelphia area. Its earliest section in the long, low lines was built around 1690. It has had several additions and a "face-lift" in 1824 by the noted Philadelphia architect William Strickland. With a magnificent garden it sits nobly on two acres of grounds with several dependencies—an icehouse, a smokehouse, and a carriage house—remaining. In the early 1700s a second house built for a married daughter was ingeniously joined to the original house at a second-floor level, leaving an open cart entrance separating them on the ground level. This cartway has now been enclosed to become a conservatory that opens into both houses, making an apartment with not one but two fireplaces! Wyck was owned and occupied by members of only one family for 283 years until it was deeded to the Wyck Charitable Trust. It is open from April to December on Tuesday, Thursday, and Saturday from 1:00 to 4:00 p.m. and other times by appointment (admission).

CLIVEDEN
6401 GERMANTOWN AVENUE
((215)848-1777)

This handsome summer residence was built by the then-Attorney General of Philadelphia, who was very active in its planning and construction. An amateur architect of good repute, he designed this elegant mansion on British lines, and it was constructed by the best Germantown workmen. The house was the center of the Battle of Germantown on October 4, 1777, and suffered severe damage. A bullet hole scar can still be seen. Members of the Chew family owned and occupied it until 1972 when it was acquired by the National Historic

Preservation Trust. Their beautiful paintings, furniture, china, and other family items have been given to the house. In 1856 a rear addition was completed adding a schoolroom and incorporating the kitchen into the main house. (Danger of fire and obnoxious cooking fumes led most larger houses to keep their cooking area quite separate from the main residence. Foods were carried through passageways to the dining room or other parts of the house.) Cliveden now serves as the regional headquarters of the National Historic Preservation Trust. The house is open from April through December, Tuesday through Saturday from 10:00 a.m. to 4:00 p.m. and on Sunday from 1:30 to 4:30 p.m. Other times are available by appointment (admission).

UPSALA
6450 GERMANTOWN AVENUE
((215)247-6113)

This handsome house was set under the tall shade trees you see today, which give it the welcome also extended by its pillared small portico. Named by its builder, John Johnson, in honor of Frederika Bremer, a Swedish author, it is a good example of Federal styles so popular in neighboring Philadelphia. The kitchen wing is older than the main house and, in the custom of the day, was a separate structure, and the unusual angle in which it has been joined to the main house is quite characteristic of Germantown architecture. It is attractively furnished, and you will want to learn more of its excellent woodwork.

It is open from April through December on Tuesday and Thursday from 1:00 to 4:00 p.m. and other times by appointment.

GERMANTOWN MENNONITE
INFORMATION CENTER
6117 GERMANTOWN AVENUE
((215)843-0943)

This is a complex of interesting variety. You can visit a Mennonite Meeting House built in 1770 for the oldest Mennonite congregation in America. The John Johnson House, built in 1768, served as a stop in the Underground Railroad in the nineteenth century. The Rittenhouse Homestead, built in 1707, was the home of William Rittenhouse, first Mennonite minister in America and owner of the first paper mill in the Colonies. (Rittenhouse Town, a mill community, is now incorporated into Fairmount Park.) Contact the Information Center *before* visiting their sites as hours vary (admission).

Deshler-Morris House
5442 Germantown Avenue
((215)596-1748)

This two-and-a-half story house resembles many other typical Germantown residences, but its interior holds a few surprises! It has had a history of receiving both friend and foe and is affectionately nicknamed the "Germantown White House" because Washington and his family took up residence there during the yellow fever epidemic of 1793 to 1794. It was also commandeered by the English Sir William Howe after the Battle of Germantown in 1777. Deeded to the United States in 1948, it is part of Independence National Historical Park and is cared for by the Germantown Historical Society. It is open April through December, Tuesday through Sunday from 1:00 to 4:00 p.m. and at other times by appointment (admission).

The Concord Schoolhouse
6309 Germantown Avenue
((215)438-6328)

This tiny one-room schoolhouse has tours by appointment only from April through October on Tuesday 10:00 a.m. to 1:00 p.m. and Thursday 1:00 to 4:00 p.m. (admission). Be sure to call first to see if they can receive you. Inside there is the original schoolmaster's desk and chair as well as other early artifacts.

Loudoun
4650 Germantown Avenue
((215)324-2877)

This handsome Greek Revival house is set on a hill and overlooks present Philadelphia. It was built in 1793 by a Philadelphia merchant, Thomas Armat, for his son and is Germantown's most lovely Federal-style house. In 1829 it was greatly enlarged, and in 1850 the portico of columns was added. Thirty-five years later the rear addition was added. Its interior furnishings and paintings belonged to the Armat and Logan families, who were joined by marriage and occupied Loudoun until 1939. This too can be seen only by appointment so call first (admission).

Stenton
18th and Windrim Streets
((215)329-7312)

William Penn's remarkable secretary, James Logan, built this early Georgian manor as a country home in 1723 to 1730. He was Chief

Justice of the Supreme Court of Pennsylvania and President of the Provincial Council, and in these various offices found himself a very busy man. You will notice many building features reminiscent of Pennsbury Mansion in this outstanding home. It is furnished with antiques from the Logan family and has an interesting history to tell. It is open varied hours, so check first.

GRUMBLETHORPE
5627 GERMANTOWN AVENUE
((215)843-4820)

This house with the intriguing name was built as a country home by John Wister and has few of the elegant touches found in other houses on the Great Road. Built in 1744, it was modernized in 1808 and its front appearance greatly altered. It, too, was taken over by British officers during the Battle of Germantown but was restored from that hard use and the deterioration of time in 1957 to 1967 by the Preservation of Landmarks Society of Philadelphia. It is open by appointment (admission).

EBENEZER MAXWELL MANSION
GREENE AND TULPEHOCKEN STREETS
((215)438-1861)

This will give you a complete change of pace and time, for here you will find a Victorian villa built in the fanciful romantic style complete with turrets and tower, round windows, painted woodwork, and tall windows of the period. It has been home to only two families since it was built in 1859 for Ebenezer Maxwell, a successful dry goods commission agent. Gardeners will enjoy the surrounding period garden too. It is Philadelphia's only mid-nineteenth-century house-museum and is attractively and appropriately furnished in period style. It is open from April through December on Wednesday and Saturday from 11:00 a.m. to 4:00 p.m. and on Sunday from 1:00 to 5:00 p.m. Appointments can also be made (admission).

As you travel Germantown Avenue, still the spine of that area, you will see how important the Great Road was in developing first independent communities which were soon linked together. When Philadelphia was the capital of Pennsylvania, the road led northwest to Bethlehem and Reading and was traveled by Indians, drovers, merchants, officials, and immigrants making their way to new homes in the New World. Before the Revolution there were regular stagecoach as well as post runs along its sturdy back, and it has never ceased to be a well-traveled route from the city to outlying suburbs and smaller towns.

It has a history of its own, joining old and new citizens from town and country in commerce and pleasure, and is well worth a daylong visit to its beautiful historic sites.

You could also combine it with a visit further up the avenue to Chestnut Hill and see how some of today's Philadelphians live.

Germantown and the Great Road is a well-kept secret!

Routing: Go north on Broad Street (Route 611) and turn left onto Route 422, Germantown Avenue or Germantown Road.

Notes

Longwood Gardens

People from every continent come to Longwood Gardens, Kennett Square, Pennsylvania, for here is one of the great estate gardens in the world and, without a doubt, the greatest one in America. It is only 30 miles from Philadelphia to this 350 acres of woodlands, wild flower preserves, magnificent trees, ranks of fountains, enormous glass-domed conservatories, and large formal gardens. It has been called the "world's greatest pleasure garden" and it truly is. The fabulous gardens were planned and produced by the late Pierre S. Du Pont, an avid gardener and a fine horticulturalist who spent long, serious hours each day with his large staff planting, pruning, and perfecting this glorious setting.

Inside the conservatories are twenty complete gardens all in an exquisite state of perfection. To keep this standard of care, the gardens, plants, shrubs, and special displays are cared for during the wee hours of the morning before the public arrives. In them are more than 14,000 different kinds of plants, roses, and orchids in bloom year round and spring blooms in the snowiest days of winter! There are planned, seasonal displays of hundreds of annuals, perennials, and exotics. Fall brings a breathless display of chrysanthemums; Christmas, literally half a thousand poinsettias; and, just when you think that spring will never arrive, there are daffodils, snowdrops, and beds of fragrant hyacinths. Throughout the summer there are many fountains throwing sparkling jets 130 feet into the air that turn into fairylike rainbows when illuminated at night with special lighting.

The arts are happily combined with the profusions of flowers with scheduled chamber music, band concerts, jazz, madrigal singers, puppets, clowns, and country dancers—a rich representation of tastes. From mid-June until September the famous illuminated fountains are presented in special displays every half hour Tuesday and Saturday evenings. Most of these take place in the Open Air Theater on the grounds, which boasts a spectacular water curtain. The Philadelphia Visitors Bureau can give you information on schedule. Ample parking and facilities are available, and admission is required.

Whether you wander outdoors, examine a new variety of your favorite rose among the hundreds of others, study the planting of the flower beds, or simply bask in the entertainment amid beautiful settings, Longwood Gardens cannot be missed! If you were not garden minded before, you will have a new understanding of this enormous and breathtaking presentation. It is one of America's great showplaces!

The Gardens at Longwood are open outdoors every day of the year from 9:00 a.m. to 6:00 p.m. From November to March they are open only until 5:00 p.m. because of early darkness. The indoor conservatories are open from 10:00 a.m. to 5:00 p.m. daily.

Routing: Take the Schuylkill Expressway west to Route 1 (City Line Avenue). Take Route 1 south to Longwood Gardens, 30 miles southwest of Philadelphia before Kennett Square. Alternatively, take I-95 south, turn left onto Route 52 to join Route 1 just north of the Gardens. The Garden entrance is well marked.

Notes

The Main Line

The Main Line is more than a railroad! It is the nickname for the local railroad, which once carried coal, lumber, and other goods to Philadelphia, New York, and other coastal ports. Several enterprising local gentlemen with prosperous investments in the line also conceived the idea of promoting its surrounding areas as the "place to live" and they succeeded.

Their commodious townhouses around Rittenhouse Square were all right for winter months, but what they really desired was a country estate for family, relatives, and long-visiting friends. Summer was long and leisurely in those days. These captains of industry had made vast fortunes in steel, lumber, coal, and iron and now regarded themselves as landed gentry.

On their large estates they raised horses, bred prize cattle, and enjoyed extensive gardens and greenhouses, orchards, and well-stocked cellars. Wives were expensively gowned by fashionable Worth of Paris, and their children were sent to the best schools in the East and South. Life was full, resplendent, and, for many, all cares were easily handled.

Their railroad ran through farmlands, acres of woods, past streams and ponds, open meadows and beside reasonable main roads. There was an excellent local and stable labor force used to good work.

French chateaus and English timbered mansions soon crowned the hills. Stables, carriage houses, pony sheds, gardens, gazebos, and tennis courts were carefully placed by the best architects. Marble, paintings, rugs and tapestries, furniture, and complete libraries were imported in those days when there were no taxes. It was rich America before World War I.

Estates needed care, and local citizens prospered too. Specialty food markets sprang up, and out-of-stock delicacies were sent for by train to

"The City" (Philadelphia or New York) to be picked up that evening at the station.

Schools, handsome churches, and pleasant clubs came next, and the area became a reasonable place to live year round. Since the summer hotels and popular boardinghouses were filled to overflowing, why not extend this?

Entrepreneurs set about widening, straightening, lighting, and enhancing the country towns and even creating new ones. Today we have a string of towns bordering the Main Line railroad that have an independent and attractive life of their own.

The best way to see them is by car. There are three centuries of history to explore in the Quaker meetinghouses, fieldstone mansions where our Founding Fathers lived or visited, some of the best schools and colleges in the United States, winding country roads, one of the largest shopping centers and its adjacent corporate center, a beautiful National Historical Park, horses galore, repertory theater, and the remarkable little Paoli Local train that runs "downtown" to Philadelphia about every half hour.

Following World War II, small houses sprouted overnight and towns swelled with business. Old houses became lawyers' or doctors' offices. Department stores opened branches and new little shops flourished. Real estate people worked twenty-nine hours a day.

Today there are no covered wagons or cattle at the drovers' inns along Lancaster Pike (Route 30), which is still the main road to the West. Take this and meander through the towns with stops here and there on the sidelines. You will be well rewarded. Remember, you are driving through the main streets and while people are most pleasant (particularly if you have map in hand), they still ride bikes home from school, leave tailgates open for loading, and chat at the crosswalks. Traffic is sparser but increasing, and there are orange school buses everywhere! A bird's-eye view of the Main Line towns follows. Each has its distinct personality.

Overbrook's apartments are sought after by commuters because of proximity to the city. Merion has attractive homes, good schools, and the Cricket Club, once a bastion of the elite. Narberth has no pretensions of elegance and is a growing small service town. Wynnewood is primarily residential with single family homes. Ardmore boasts the first shopping center in the United States and has a good supply of churches. Haverford is home to a Quaker college and attractive living. Bryn Mawr is almost completely immersed in the world of academe with its excellent women's college and preparatory schools. Rosemont and Villanova have colleges developed for Roman Catholic curriculae. Their students add a lively note to the streets and trains, as you will see. St. David's, primarily a post office and train stop, has a Welsh name reminding us of the settlers who developed this region. Strafford and Wayne is an area for newer homes, and Devon sprawls over the countryside with larger, older summer residences. Berwyn is another business center with an Italian background, and Daylesford (nicknamed "tiny town" by railroad conductors) is a new development on an old estate. Paoli was once the end of the line with railroad yards, but, as population hurried into the country, it has become another hub for services. Malvern and Exton grow beyond.

Start out book in hand, but leave plenty of time to stop and look at regional architecture (estates, campuses, and churches), eat at some of the good, little restaurants, visit Valley Forge Park, or wind along some of the parallel roads to see the countryside.

These smaller towns reflect the special character of Philadelphia in a hundred ways!

Routing: Take the Schuylkill Expressway west to City Line Avenue (Route 1). Take City Line Avenue south to Route 30 and west on Route 30 to Exton or beyond.

Notes

Notes

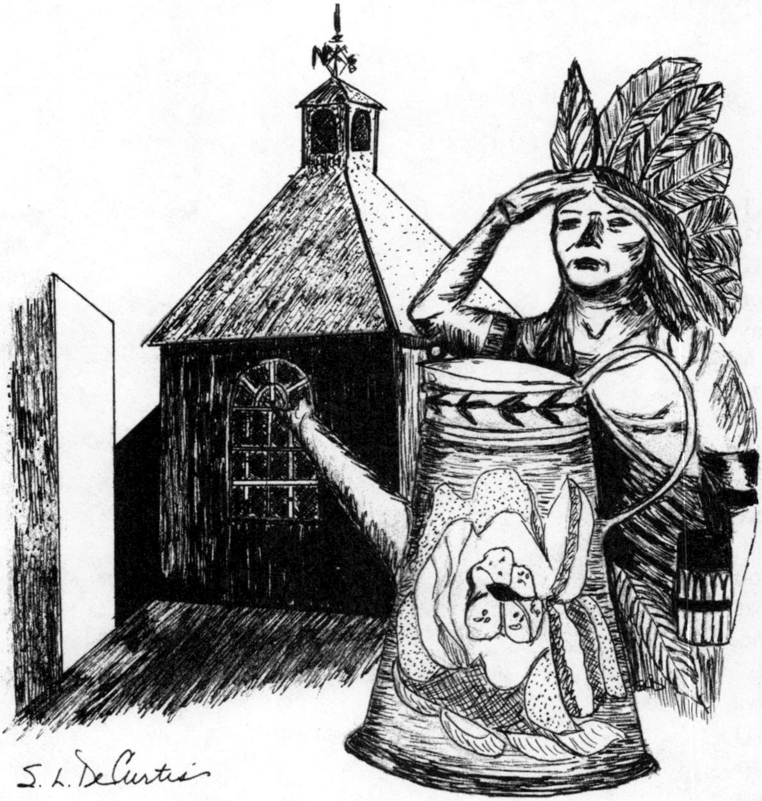
S. L. DeCurtis

The Mercer Mile

The life of Henry Chapman Mercer spanned the years of 1856 to 1930, days when the Industrial Revolution changed the workplace and face of the country. His death at the beginning of the Great Depression marked the time affluent eras ended and Americans changed their ways of thought and behavior.

Mercer's vision was of the so-called "common man"—the day laborer, the tradesman, the farmer, and the anonymous American whose day-to-day routines built the backbone of the country.

An archeologist and an historian with a trained and sensitive eye, Mercer soon saw that the tools of many trades and skills were fast becoming extinct. He scoured old barns, attics, derelict taverns, sheds, and country stores and began a collection of representative useful "tools of the nation makers," as he put it. In discarded and worn signs, posters, hand-forged machinery parts, plows, pitchforks, spinning wheels, toys, and decorative arts, he saw a vanishing reflection of us all. These he collected and finally housed in a museum of his own advanced design and construction.

The museum, housing sawmill and lumbering tools, coopering and carpentry tools, and those used in skilled shipbuilding, rose as a creation of turrets and towers. Outside large tools were housed in sheds and barns. Soon the coaches, carriages, wagons, and carts of transportation history joined them, followed by the necessary utensils for medicine, a printshop, fire fighting, and other community professions. Tavern signs, shop figures, ice-harvesting tools—the collection continued to grow until it was hailed as a "national treasure" by James Michener, himself a Bucks County native. Today this vast collection is assembled and open to the public in Doylestown, Bucks County, Pennsylvania.

In addition, the large mansion, Fonthill, Mercer's unusual home, is now open to the public for scheduled guided tours. Its forty rooms are strongly decorated with ceramic tiles and mosaics, which also intrigued Mercer. He founded and operated his own tile works, specializing in original designs formed from his own "recipe" still used today. The Columbus Room with its vaulted ceiling and the theme of tiles depicting the New World testifies to this pursuant interest.

The Mercer Mile consists of the large indoor-outdoor museum complex with its research library and good museum shop; the enormous mansion, Fonthill; and the Moravian Pottery and Tile Works close by.

The museum is open March through December, Monday through Saturday from 10:00 a.m. to 4:30 p.m. and Sunday from 1:00 to 4:00 p.m.. Tours are scheduled with a trained guide (admission). Fonthill is open at the same time and hours. There are tours, with the last one scheduled to leave at 3:30 p.m. ((215)345-0201).

The Mercer Mile is completed with the Moravian Tile Works, which is still turning out beautiful ceramics. It is open to the public Wednesday through Sunday from 10:00 a.m. to 5:00 p.m., with the last guided tour leaving at 4:00 p.m. ((215)345-6722). The buildings are closed during January and February. All are closed on Easter, Thanksgiving, and Christmas.

This is a unique museum of general and special interests set in the heart of a beautiful rural countryside. You are near Pearl Buck's Green Hills Farm and also the village of the New Hope, both of which can complete an interesting day (see text).

Routing: Go north on Broad Street to Route 611 and continue north to Doylestown. The museum and Fonthill are on South Main Street and are marked. The Moravian Tile Works is nearby on Swamp Road, Route 313.

Notes

Mill Grove

The beautiful country home of John James Audubon now houses a museum devoted to his works and his life in the wooded area beside a stream that lured the country's first naturalist from the duty with which his French father had charged him. In 1804 the French sea captain, Jean Audubon, sent his son, born in 1785 in San Domingo (now Haiti), to oversee the lead mines that he owned beyond Philadelphia.

The house, built in 1782, overlooked broad meadows, the Perkiomen Creek, hills, and small valleys running with wildlife. The young man spent his days roaming the countryside with a sketchbook and notepad in hand. Watercolors, oils, drawings, and sketches of flowers, birds, and small animals soon filled a large portfolio. Many of these had never before been drawn from life.

In 1806 the mine and estate were sold to Audubon's partner, and John James married Lucy Bakewell of Fatlands, a neighboring plantation. This loyal wife spent the rest of her life encouraging the young artist, often supporting them both as they moved about the country, her reward being the works he drew with unsurpassed accuracy, color, and naturalness.

It was 1828 before his engravings were finally printed in London and hand-colored by one R. Havell. Soon many works were thus reproduced for sale, and a first edition of octavo size was introduced by Mr. J. J. Bowen of Philadelphia. They are displayed at Mill Grove with a charming drawing of Audubon himself by his brother-in-law. Also on display are the original copperplate, writings, letters, and a 1928 photograph of Mill Grove.

Among his friends he numbered not only other naturalists and explorers but foremost scientists and men of letters of his day, who came to realize that this self-trained artist was one to be recognized.

The house is set at the end of a long tree-lined drive with a square, stone barn at one side. Birds twitter and call year round on the nature trails and meadows.

Inside, some rooms are furnished in Audubon's period, and among the most striking features are the hand-painted murals on the downstairs walls. The third floor shows his workplace with a canoe, baskets for gathering specimens, a sled for the Canadian journeys he took, and the iron kettle used for washing both his clothes and animal species on his long trips. His western trips with Indians and frontiersmen called for the leather bags and trunks that could be used in camp or on the trail when he observed wildlife at dawn or dusk feeding hours.

On the trails of Mill Grove there are winter and summer feeding stations, nesting boxes, and the plantings that invite more than 175 species of birds and 400 species of plants.

Bring your camera and your own sketch pad in the winter solitude or flourishing summer months. The curator and staff are glad to answer questions and tell you of special events.

Mill Grove is open daily except Monday from 10:00 a.m. to 5:00 p.m. It is closed on Thanksgiving, Christmas, and New Year's Day ((215)666-5593). No admission is charged.

Routing: Take the Schuylkill Expressway west to Route 202. Take Route 202 south to the Betzwood Bridge exit. Go west to Route 363. Follow Route 363 north to Audubon Road and turn right. There are signs for Mill Grove.

Notes

Morven

In 1701 in what is present-day Princeton, New Jersey, Quaker Richard Stockton, lawyer and civic leader, purchased from William Penn 5,500 acres of "goode lands in The Jersies." In 1755 his grandson built a Georgian mansion that was dubbed Morven by a later mistress of the estate.

Another Richard Stockton, then owner and also a Quaker supporting the Colonial cause, was forced to abandon his position as member of the Royal Governor's Council and the Supreme Court of the colony. After its capture by the British, the estate Morven was commandeered by General Cornwallis as his British military headquarters. At his departure the place was looted, badly vandalized, and partially burned.

In the humid summer of 1783 Princeton was designated the home of the new Continental Congress, and Morven became the White House of its day as the president of the Congress, Elias Boudinot, used the house for much elegant and political entertaining. Washington, lodged nearby at Rocky Hill, was a frequent visitor in its spacious dining room and formal parlor.

Morven was later altered and enlarged by two wings and a new piazza. After another fire in 1821, Greek-Revival cornices and demilune windows were added, along with interior reeded arches, new mantels, and fashionable plaster walls.

The naval hero Richard Field Stockton eventually inherited both house and land, but at his death it was conveyed to another branch of the family to repay debts. The house was then returned to a more simple style and some of the surrounding land sold. A Philadelphia architect John Nottman added appendages in the rear and a Tuscan portico. In 1928 the house was rented to an outsider, who added a swimming pool and a tennis court with other modernizations. Morven remained a Stockton family property until 1945, when it became the property of the State of New Jersey. Subsequently, it has played host to many leading political figures, including President Kennedy and President Carter, and kings and queens.

Guides recount the history of the Empire dining room table and its sixteen rare matching chairs and the large silver fruit bowl. There is also a handomse Stockton painting by Thomas Sully and a lovely cherry highboy believed to have been a present from Washington to Richard Stockton III.

It is best to call Morven before you go as it also serves as the headquarters of the Historical Society and sometimes has special events ((609)683-1069).

This is the time to see the lovely college town of Princeton and the Thomas Clarke House on Mercer Street. In nearby Laurenceville, another academic town, there is an interesting white brick Presbyterian church first organized in 1698, one of the oldest in America.

Routing: Go north on I-95 and cross the Delaware River into New Jersey. Continue north on I-95 and exit at Route 206. Follow 206 north to Princeton. The mansion is on the left before you enter the town.

Notes

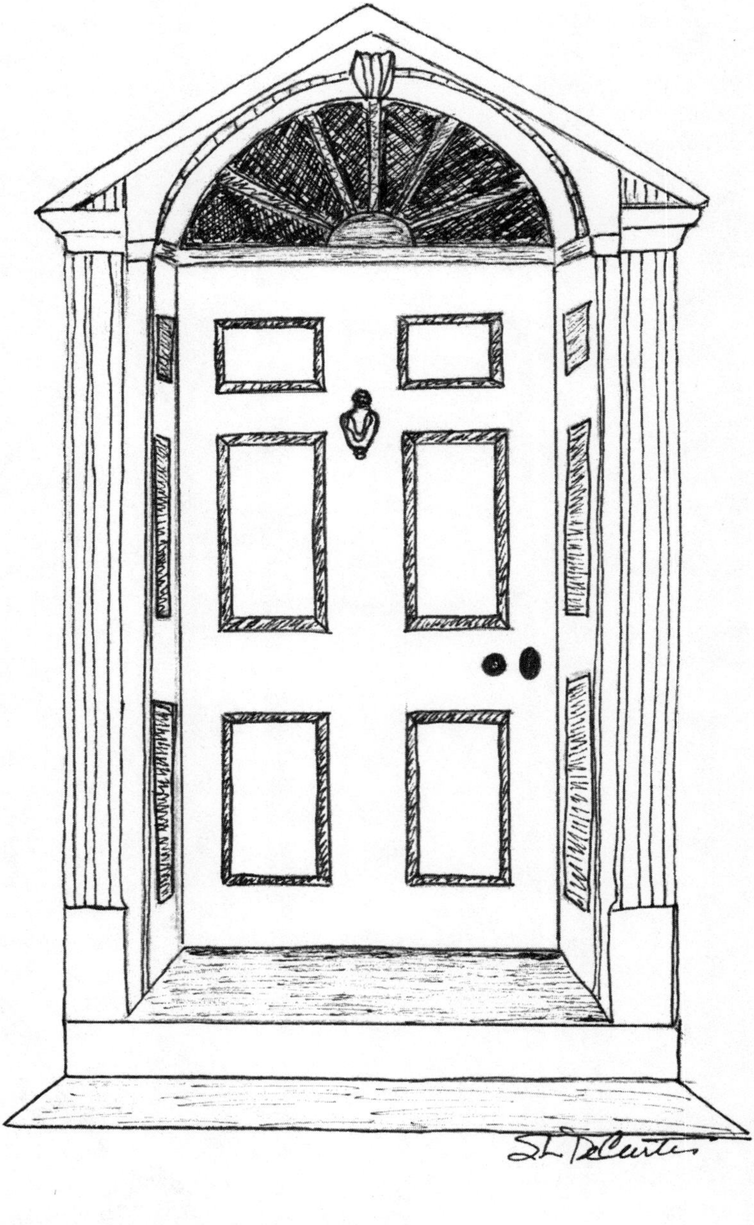

New Castle

This little town, a quiet mirror of Colonial, Federal, and some Victorian architecture, lies as it always did, snugly on the banks of the Delaware River. It has had a tumultuous and important history under four flags: Dutch, Swedish, English, and American; as a fort, a seaport, and a market and court town. Old New Castle was a Colonial as well as a state capital, and one of the major ports of entry into the new country.

Long before William Penn came ashore in 1682 to take his first footsteps in the New World, both the Swedes and the Dutch had built forts at this location. Bold Peter Stuyvesant himself marched down from New Amsterdam (now New York) to establish Fort Casimir where a small Swedish settlement had already taken root. The Swedes soon recaptured it and named it Fort Trinity. Because the Dutch already had vast holdings of lands for hundreds of miles along the Hudson River and also in what is now New Jersey, they once again recaptured the fort and placed it under the protection of this great colony called New Amstel.

English lands and settlers were both north and south of this location, so in 1664 nervous King Charles II sent two armed merchant ships, which speedily completed their mission of taking over the beleaguered settlement. They promptly named it New Castle and started the town on its prosperous way. Brick kilns were built, metal smiths and ironmongers set to work, carpenters were busy seven days a week, and nearby fields bloomed with grain easily milled on the spot.

To William Penn's amazement, as he took possession of the enormous grant of land awarded him by the king, all seemed well. He claimed all of what is now Pennsylvania, the Lower Three Counties of Delaware, and all the land within a 12-mile circle around New Castle.

These he took possession of in the "livery of the seizin," according to an old ceremony accepting "turf, twig, soyl, and water."

It was now Lord Baltimore's time to protest from the French colony of Maryland. He argued for years in bitter anger over this "presumptuous claiming," but the Quaker Penn fostered only peace and plenty in the growing port. It was 1704 before he granted the Three Lower Counties of Delaware their own assemblies.

With the news of the Battle of Lexington, the Colonists prepared for war. They had long petitioned King George, had appointed delegates to the 1775 Continental Congress, and well knew the mood of the restless country. George Read and Thomas McKean of New Castle were both signers of the Declaration of Independence, and the area soon raised a goodly militia to send to Washington in New York. When a large naval flotilla anchored off nearby Head of Elk preparing to capture Philadelphia, the president of Delaware sought refuge on a ship lying at the New Castle docks, carrying with him the state seal and important documents. He was captured, and the government was forced to reconvene in Dover to the south.

New Castle's history lay claim to an even more prosperous one when in 1852 it became the terminus of the popular New Castle-Frenchtown Railroad. This replaced onerous stagecoach traffic to the Chesapeake Bay and the South and soon eclipsed the coastwise packets from Philadelphia and New England. But the selection of Wilmington for the main railroad lines finally sounded the death knell of large commerce in little New Castle.

This is to us a happy circumstance, for it has preserved a complete town which is a joy to the casual visitor, an architectural fancier, or one interested in early American history. It presents a composite picture of Dutch, French, Colonial, Georgian, Federal, and Empire features.

There are many beautiful restored large and small homes, public buildings, churches, and tree-lined streets. The long Village Green and its market stalls are still there. The old armory for storage of ammunition is now a restaurant, but the little alleys of the Strand are used as passageways today. The shops and the White Swan Inn are delightful so pick up a walking tour map at one of them. There is good food at all prices even on the riverbank where you can picnic in the park.

New Castle Day is held annually on the third Sunday in May, and at Christmastime there are Candlelight Walking Tours with visits in some of the old houses decorated for the season.

An easy 35 miles from Philadelphia, old New Castle is not to be missed! For written information contact the Delaware State Travel Service, Delaware Development Office, 99 Kings Highway, Dover, Delaware 19901 ((800)441-8846)

Routing: Go east to I-95 and take I-95 south through Wilmington. Turn east on Route 141 into old New Castle.

Notes

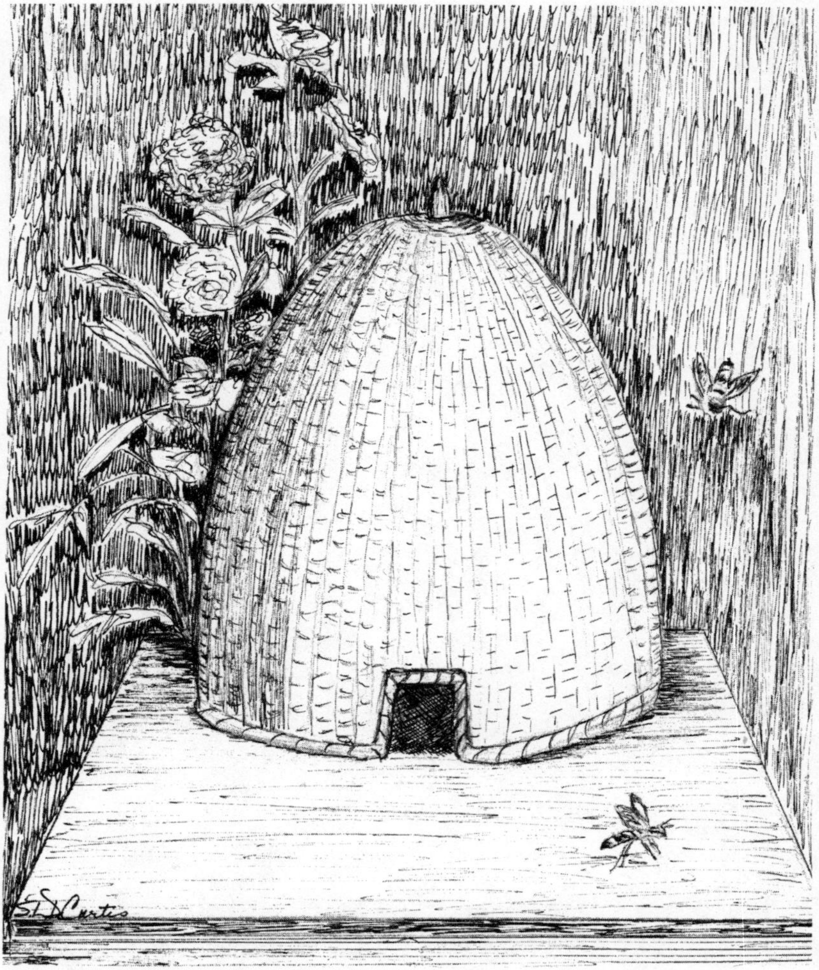
S.L.D. Curtis

Pennsbury Manor

We have all heard of the remarkable "new thought" advocated by young William Penn in England in the 1600s.

This remarkable, visionary man, who spent time in European jails for promotion of his ideas, left the world a legacy so varied that we tend to find it overshadowed by our picture of him as the gentle Quaker, founder of Pennsylvania in the New World.

In 1681 King Charles of England owed the Penn family an enormous debt and thus awarded him as a "friend of the Court" a charter for lands extending west from the Delaware River and bounded by New York and Maryland. With this designation, William Penn became the largest English landowner in history!

Fortunately, this man, who advocated "Let us see what Love can do" rather than resorting to threats, lawsuits, or martial arts in settling disputes, was a man of ideals as well as practicality.

It was William Penn who laid out a long-range projection for a government with a legislative assembly elected by suffrage rather than inheritance or indulgence to a regal whim. His was the first council to be appointed by an elected governor. His new criminal code dispensed with the many cruel punishments levied for capital crimes in England. His codification marked only two crimes—treason and murder—with a death penalty.

His Holy Experiment gave us the heritage of religious freedom, and he advocated honest and humane dealings with the American Indians when many in surrounding areas were greedily appropriating their lands, disclaiming fishing and hunting rights, and ignoring trade agreements made with these natural Americans.

Pennsbury Manor was built reflecting the great country estates of England with which Penn was so familiar. The site on the banks of the Delaware was in easy distance by road and boat from Philadelphia, and a visit to this excellent reconstruction gives an accurate, well-rounded picture of how land holdings of this size were planned and run domestically.

He showed with justifiable pride his imported Red Devon cows, Dorset sheep, and fine horses, and all the community knew "Tammerlane" with affection for the Arabian gelding that carried him hundreds of miles through the countryside. Guests and official visitors enjoyed many walks in his formal English parterre gardens and long lawns stretching down to the Delaware where his own commuting barge and boats were moored.

The grounds are extensive and well cared for from the entrance drive to the furthest orchard. The house is a lovely one, and you are free to explore the grounds at your own pace. Here are a bake and brew house, kitchen gardens, herb and flower gardens, orchards, fruit bushes, and a vineyard carefully placed near his bee skep.

Picnicking in good weather is welcomed at Pennsbury Manor, and there are many special events planned each month of the year. You will enjoy a Market Fair Day, see sheepshearing, Colonial stenciling, or sign up for a genealogy workshop. Holidays are always observed with special decorations, and sometimes there are Candlelight Tours and musical events. Call ahead and see what the staff is planning while you visit.

This visit is a good one to accompany a visit to nearby historic Fallsington where William Penn was always a welcome visitor and attendant at Quaker meetings.

Pennsbury is open weekdays from 9:00 a.m. to 5:00 p.m. and Sunday from 12:00 noon to 5:00 p.m. It is closed on Monday. Admission is charged. For more information call (215)946-0400. For brochures, write to 400 Pennsbury Memorial Lane, Morrisville, Pennsylvania 19067.

Routing: Take I-95 north and exit at the Bristol exit. Take Route 413 north about 1 mile. Exit at Route 13 and go east. Follow signs on Route 13 to Pennsbury Manor.

Notes

Peter Wentz Farmstead

Situated in the countryside about 20 miles from Philadelphia is the fieldstone mansion of Peter Wentz, who engaged in active farming and obviously prospered well.

On a rise overlooking a neighboring valley, the house is surrounded by its large red barn with traditional space for animals below and threshing floor above, a pigsty, an old orchard, sown fields, a kitchen and herb garden, and a grapevine thought to be the original and still bearing. A pump with its stone trough and a series of half or "Dutch" doors bespeak of the sturdy German background of Wentz families. An inscribed blessing on stone is set by the front door and can be translated from the German by your guide.

Built in 1758 by his father, a successful German privateer, the house stands in the Georgian manner with a formal front and more simply designed sides. A small square balcony overlooks the front door, and a pent eave shades the windows of the first floor.

The house has been meticulously restored by Montgomery County, and the surprising interiors are based on accurate research by professionals well acquainted with the area's styles, colors, and manner of living. The grounds are entered by a walkway between split rail snake fences. Sheep wander in the large meadow, an orchard blooms in the spring, and a typical cross-barred garden now grows vegetables and flowers with the herbs known to have been appropriate. Both outside and inside are carefully kept in the somewhat surprising bright colors of the original paint, which was found intact on many walls. This paint represents true Pennsylvania colors rather than the more familiar Williamsburg gray-greens and blues. The striking decorative polka-dot sponge painting was intact in many places, as were the blue and salmon colors still untouched in the Washington room!

Much attention is given to the kitchen and particularly the upstairs rooms occupied on two occasions by Washington as his headquarters. Here he was well cared for, with meals prepared under guarded conditions for fear of poisoning. A comfortable bedroom and a large room with a wall of closets across the hall served as his office. Two other rooms may have been used by his aides. It is believed that here the plans for the Battle of Germantown were set. Furnishings are not original to the house but are accurate for the period and locale. An interesting feature is the two five-plate stoves in the dining room and the master bedroom. A short film on the history and local artifacts in the exhibit area provides a good introduction to a visit within the house.

Talented weavers, cooks, and other craftsmen demonstrate their arts at scheduled times, and many seasonal events are planned throughout the year. There is a good museum shop in the barn with well-made and well-priced folk art objects for sale.

After you see some of the more elegant historic houses in this four-state area, the Peter Wentz Farmstead adds another dimension to learning of the varied people in the Pennsylvania area.

The Farmstead is open Tuesday through Saturday from 10:00 a.m. to 4:00 p.m. and Sunday from 1:00 to 4:00 p.m. Admission is free, but donations to the Furnishing Fund are welcome.

Routing: Take the Schuylkill Expressway west to Route 202. Go south on Route 202 to the Betzwood Bridge exit. Go west to Route 363. Take Route 363 north to Route 73. Turn right at Route 73. Follow Route 73 to the first intersection and turn left into the farmstead.

Notes

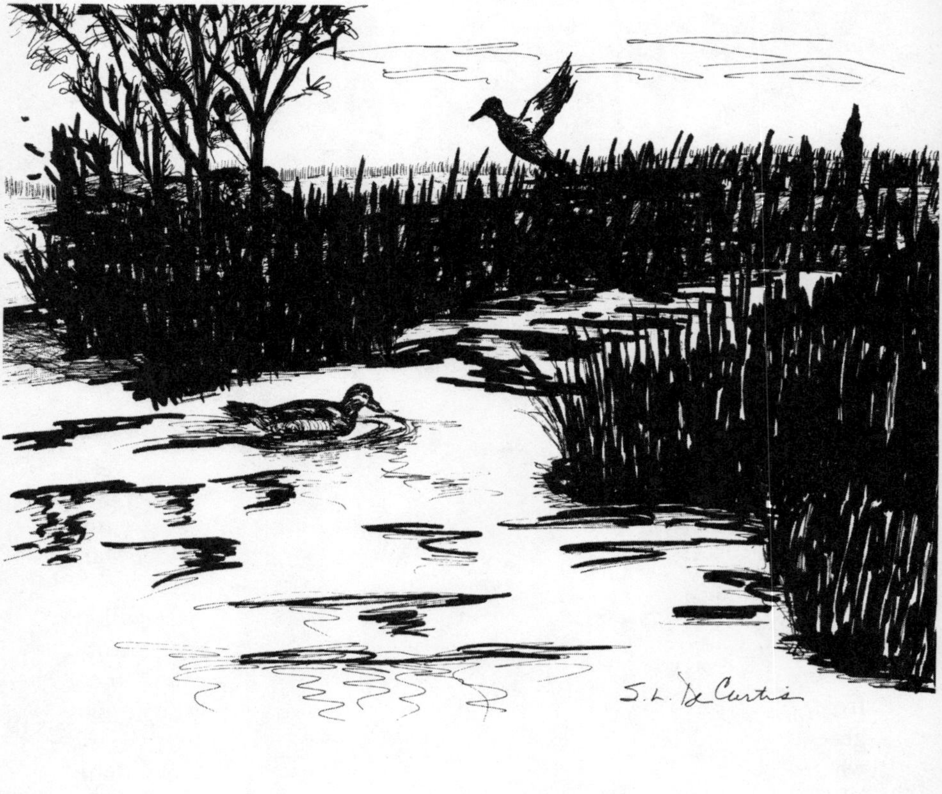
S.L. DeCurtis

The Pine Barrens

The Pine Barrens, affectionately known as the "Pines," occupies one quarter of the entire State of New Jersey and lies across the Delaware River from Philadelphia. This remote spot lies halfway between Boston and Virginia, and few people outside of the region know it. Its forest, swamps, bogs, hills, unmarked roads, streams, and rivers are wonderful and rewarding exploring. Go by car or canoe, and, if you have a chance, fly above it. You will hardly believe your eyes! After a visit you may wonder why you have not known or heard more of this area.

By canoe enter one of its rivers—the Mullica, Batsto, Maurice, or Wading—and in the stillness of the ancient wilderness it will be hard to realize that you are not far from the Atlantic City Expressway! Stop at one of the Information Centers, and, if you plan to go deeper into this land, seek out a ranger for explicit directions. They do not want you to get lost!

The Pine Barrens geological phenomenon was created 400 million years ago when volcanic mountains were worn down by the Atlantic Ocean surge and today's Appalachians were a sea separating them from the mainland that lay farther west. Erosion of weather and gradual deposits of rocky sediments in this sea created a vast swamp where 300 million years ago jungles of giant ferns and bracken flourished. Two hundred million years ago lava again created the hills and mountains of New Jersey and dinosaurs roamed, feasting on succulent vegetation. Trees arose and bright birds flourished in the almost tropical climate. One million years ago the Ice Age descended, but the Pine Barrens remained beyond the limits of its grasping fingers. In this great battle of Nature, Atlantic seawater dropped 300 feet leaving a land bridge from New Jersey to Newfoundland. Because of this we see today vegetation unique to the Pine Barrens.

An enormous aquifer still feeds the streams that flow to the sea. This lake is said to be equal to a lake 75 feet deep and 1,000 miles square with a constant temperature of 54 degrees. Here are mysterious trees such as dwarf pines only as high as a man's waist and curly grass-fern, almost never seen elsewhere. Goldcrest blooms; its nearest relative is in Australia. Mosses flourish that do not appear again until Florida or South Africa, and you can walk on acres of bogs or sphagnum moss. Ferns abound along with lilies, swamp azalea, wild magnolia, and twenty-three kinds of orchids.

Today it is the scene of vanished towns and the shy, self-sufficient people who choose to live there. Colonial stage routes from New York to the South are the dirt tracks used today, and the place called Washington, where five roads meet to form a star, was once a busy town. Names like Mt. Misery, Apple Pie Hill, Jenkins Neck, and Hog Wallow are gone too, though once they were havens for Tories who fled here from the Revolution. After the war Quakers made their homes here with Hessian soldiers, Huguenots, and Leni-Lenape Indians finding shelter and food in the fish, wild berries, and small wildlife.

The Welsh, Scots, and English soon found the water rich with iron peat, and furnaces sprang up that poured out cannonballs for the Revolution and the War of 1812. Later industries supplying iron for firebacks, lanterns, tools, wheel rims, and fencing did a good business in the Barrens. Paper was made from salt-marsh grass and glass fashioned for the sparkling chandeliers all along the coast.

It was the railroad that sounded the death knell to the villages with their taverns, inns, churches, and schools as steam and coal replaced charcoal as fuel. One by one the furnaces died out. Privateering became a lucrative way of life with the seizing of ships carrying molasses, teak, sugarcane or spices from the Caribbean. These were carried to an inland cove or deep into the Barrens to be divided as spoils.

Today the Pine Barrens are rife with the sound of whippoorwills, nighthawks, jays, chats, and larks. Owls whir above the sandy soil preying on small animals, and the great bald eagle knows where to nest. One of Nature's prizes is the brilliant tree frog whose green and purple skin lures naturalists from around the world.

The wonderful part of the Pine Barrens is that it is there for you to explore. The Wharton Tract, Lebanon Forest, or Bass River State Forest are easily reached. Study a New Jersey map and with your canoe or bikes on the car roof, cross the Delaware and relax in a natural setting that is trying hard not to give way to high rises, town houses, and supermarkets.

Routing: Go north on Broad Street to Vine Street and turn right. Follow Vine Street to the Benjamin Franklin Bridge. Cross the bridge and go to Route 70. Follow Route 70 south to Route 206. Go south on Route 206 toward Hammonton and into the Pine Barren area.

Notes

The Poconos

The wooded, mountainous region north of Philadelphia has been a vacation haven for more than 100 years as popular as the "Shore." It will attract anyone who loves old, grand hotels and outdoor sports of any season, for there are skating, skiing, swimming, and boating with resort hotels at all prices year round. They all offer package rates for special events and attractions that can surely unwind weary bones. Check the ads in *The Philadelphia Inquirer* Travel Section on a Sunday, or write or call the Pocono Mountain Vacation Bureau at 1004 Main Street, Stroudsburg, Pennsylvania 18360-1695 ((717)421-5791). Any travel agent can also give information and make reservations.

There are large hotels, smaller inns, lodges, motels, cottages, timesharing apartments and town houses, or campgrounds that take trailers or vans. The state parks have good accommodations, and there are privately operated campgrounds that offer lakeside fun. Bigger resorts and restaurants have piano bars, dancing, and entertainment. There are also some dinner theaters. Many offer sports instruction at all levels and ages, and some offer baby-sitting with a vacation for Mom!

Year round there is lots to do. In winter try slope or cross-country skiing or a snowmobile park. Ice skating indoors or out is good at any age, followed by a pool swim (in, not out!), saunas, or exercise rooms. For spectator sports ask about winter carnivals. Horseback riding year round is good on marked trails, and some resorts have sleigh rides, fun for the entire family who jog along to the sound of bells under a fur lap robe. In warm weather there are tennis, golf, swimming, boating, fishing, or sailing plus several places you can raft. Seasonal events bring hayrides, steam train rides, white water trips, laurel blossom festivals with pretty local queens, art shows, auctions, antique car exhibits, singing, dancing, theater, and even a band concert.

If you do not want all that activity, browse at Grey Towers mansion and remember "how it was then" or tour the rural farm near Stroudsburg at Quiet Valley Living Historical Farm on Route 209 south ((717)992-6161). Hours vary with seasons. In Bushkill learn more about the remarkable Delaware Indians at the Pocono Indian Museum with their artifacts, weapons, tools, and chronological explanation of this great tribe. This too is on Route 209 ((717)588-9338).

There are fun and interest for all and, best of all, they are only a few hours away from Philadelphia on main roads.

Routing: Take the Schuylkill Expressway west to the Pennsylvania Turnpike. Go east on the Turnpike to Route 9, the Northeast Extension. Follow the Northeast Extension north to the Poconos.

Notes

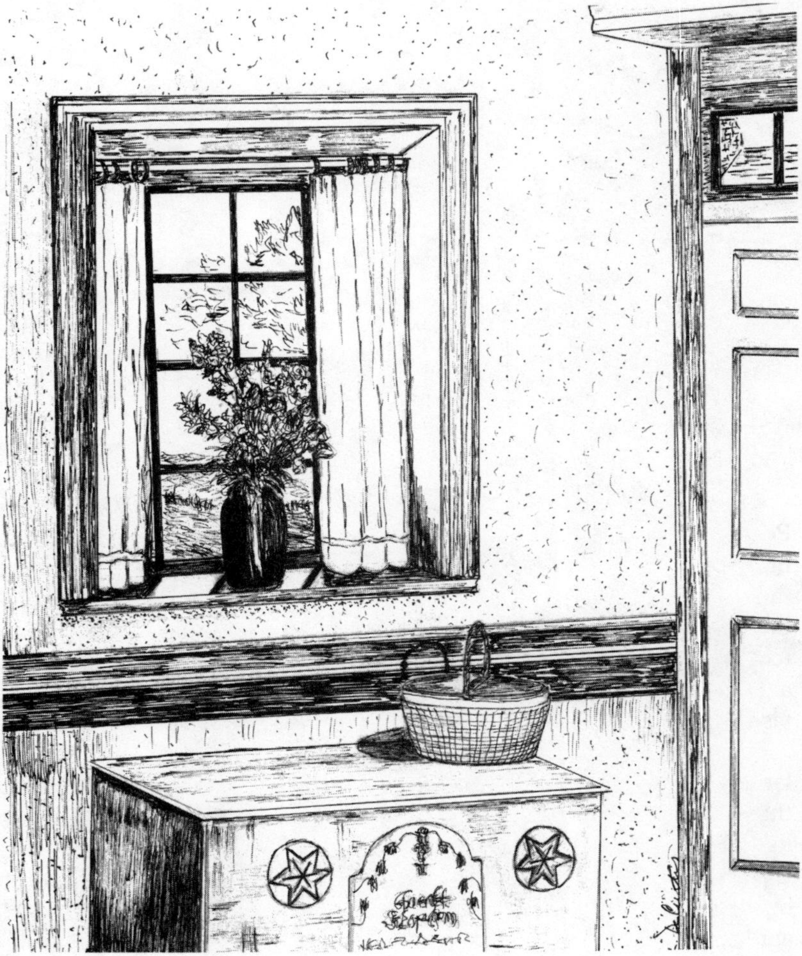

Pottsgrove

At the edge of the town he founded in 1750 sits Pottsgrove, the late Georgian mansion of John Potts, Ironmaster. Built in the Quaker tradition of the best materials, it is an architectural gem of its day fronted in sandstone with a wide double door overlooking the Schuylkill River. At one time there was quite a settlement for this self-contained little community, for around the house were tenant houses, a paymaster's house, a gristmill and storehouses, a brewery, and the sheds and barns for farming. All have now disappeared with the growth of Pottstown.

Inside there are many evidences of refined and elegant living, for Potts was one of the wealthiest men around Philadelphia and host to important people. He received his guests in the wide front hall before taking them to the formal parlor carefully finished with crown moldings, a paneled fireplace, and tea table set for use. Across the hall is a formal dining room with a long extension table for festive parties and a Rembrandt Peale portrait of Washington, who is believed to have visited here often.

Behind that room is an informal dining room to accommodate his large family of thirteen children plus a tutor who might well have used that schoolmaster's desk. The original kitchen opens off this room with its brick floor, beamed ceiling, and huge fireplace where the cooking was done over the open fire. We see a handy cupboard, usually stocked in his day with pies, cakes, jams, and jellies all made from his own gardens. Outside was the "necessary," a smokehouse, and a springhouse for "refrigerated" storage.

A wide, graceful staircase leads to four rooms on the upper floor. The master bedroom and dressing room looks out to the plantation's river docks, where mules and their cargo journeyed to Philadelphia. Since it was often the custom to entertain friends or do business in the bedroom, it is comfortably furnished, as is the second bedroom, which has an unusual tent-bed that could be disassembled for traveling. Its painted indoor shutters are an unusual feature and add a colorful note. The third bedroom is furnished as a children's room with a rocking horse, a toy cradle, and a small four-poster bed over which is a hand-sewn coverlet. Other children's rooms lie in the third but unopened story of the house.

As you descend, there is an interesting room that may well have served as Potts's office. It is now furnished with charming portraits and interesting documents, one of which is a certificate of marriage.

This handsome house well represents the wealthy manner of good living attained by many prosperous, industrious men of the 1700s who also found time to serve in many offices of their new and growing country.

Pottsgrove is open Wednesday through Saturday from 9:00 a.m. to 5:00 p.m. and Sunday from 12:00 noon to 5:00 p.m. Admission is charged ((215)326-4014).

Routing: Take the Schuylkill Expressway west to the Pennsylvania Turnpike. Go west on the Turnpike to Exit 23. Go north on Route 23 to Route 100. Pottsgrove is near the later section of Route 422 at Route 100.

Notes

The Pusey Plantation

Landingford was its original name when it belonged to Caleb Pusey, and it is the last remaining house where William Penn was known to have visited in Pennsylvania when he established his Holy Experiment.

In 1682 Pusey assumed manorship of the Chester Mills, the first sawmill and gristmill set up by Penn himself. When he visited a second time, the decorative weather vane bearing his initials was forged with the date of 1699 and still swings in the wind. There is also evidence that Washington well knew of this mill, as did Anthony Wayne of Waynesborough, for the general ordered its millstones to be carefully buried before the advancing British arrived in Philadelphia.

The old stone house was constructed in 1683 and has been carefully restored with good documentation, as it is believed to be the oldest British-built house in the Commonwealth. The first mill was prefabricated in England and shipped here to be set up on the creek, where its two towers were later victims of high seasonal floods. A single-room dwelling was discovered where the Colonial herb garden now is, and it is thought that Pusey first lived here.

The house originally had a fireplace for cooking and warmth with the back of the oven outside, but in 1699 this was included in the inside of the house as it was slightly enlarged. The windows are tiny, for each pane of glass was subject to taxing; but inside-bolted shutters added to warmth and safety. There is a sleeping loft above, but access was by a movable ladder pulled up after the sleepers.

There is an 1839 schoolhouse with interesting artifacts inside, including an old spoon bearing the initials of Ann and Caleb Pusey in the old-fashioned manner. The log house built for Pusey's great-great-granddaughter still stands, having been moved here for preservation. There is also a Lancaster County barn, a vegetable and flower garden, and a picnicking area with a parking lot.

The Pusey Plantation is open Saturday and Sunday from 1:00 to 4:00 p.m., May through September (admission).

Routing: Take I-95 south and exit at Widener College in Chester, following signs to Crozer-Chester Medical Center on Upland Avenue. Look very carefully for Pusey Plantation signs!

Notes

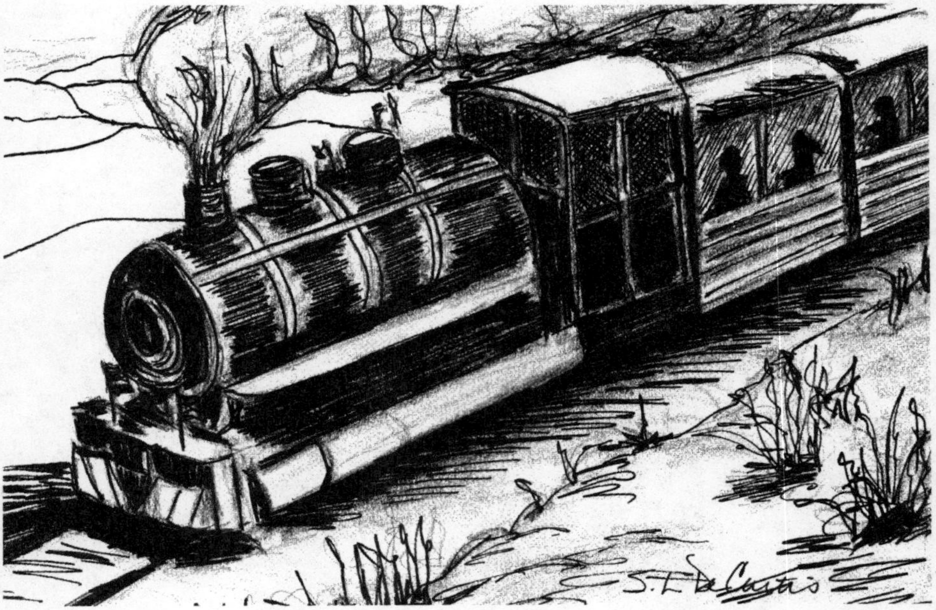

Railroading

There are several ways you can go with railroads. You may opt for rides and special events on real trains, visits to the wondrous exhibitions of model and miniature trains, or visits to the excellent transportation or train museums.

In more and more parts of the country bona fide railroad travel is disappearing, leaving long faces and longer memories staring down the empty tracks after the final caboose. Fortunately, the American spirit of nostalgia plus ingenuity has saved many engines, passenger cars, freight cars, tracks, signals, and stations from complete extinction.

Within a day's trip from Philadelphia you can ride both steam or diesel cars that are gloriously again varnished, polished, and shined to perfection to operate on fixed and printed schedules. Or you can become engrossed in the art of miniature railroading, that art of small-scale models running perfectly on little tracks through tunnels, blowing at tiny water towers, and roaring over hills and valleys that seem real.

Pennsylvania, New Jersey, and Delaware all have "big" trains you can ride. Pine Creek Railroad has a short ride on a historic steam- and diesel-powered passenger line in Allaire State Park in New Jersey only a few miles from points of shore interest. Their timetable has multiple choices, including trips every thirty minutes, special trips for school groups, a Great Locomotive Chase, Civil War reenactment, Railroaders Day in early September, and a Christmas Express with Santa Claus. For full information call the New Jersey Museum of Transportation (201)938-5524. Allaire State Park is located on Route 524 in Wall Township, only 2 miles east of the Garden State Parkway, Exit 98, and 1 mile east of I-95, Exit 31.

There there is popular old East Broad Top, which will give you a 10 mile, 50-minute ride on one of the oldest narrow-gauge tracks in

America. This line was built in 1873 to move coal from the mines of central Pennsylvania and was in operation until 1956. It is now run by the U.S. Department of the Interior and is designated as an historic landmark. In addition to the ride, you can go in the roundtable and walk right up to the old steam engines. There are films, postcards, and souvenirs to remind you that you have been there, and at the end of the line there is a picnic grove where you can stop for lunch before you reboard the train to return. From Philadelphia, head for Rock Hill Furnace via the Pennsylvania Turnpike, traveling west to Interchange Number 14, Willow Hill. Then go north on Route 75 to Spring Run Road. Take Route 641 to Shade Gap and Route 522 to Orbisonia. If you want a brochure in advance, write East Broad Top Railroad, Rockhill Furnace, Pennsylvania 17249 ((814)447-3011). This attraction is beyond Harrisburg and about halfway to Bradford if you are looking at a map.

The Strasburg Railroad is closer to Philadelphia, being in the Amish country off Route 30 before you reach Lancaster. The countryside is lovely, particularly in spring and fall. Bring your camera on this one. You will take a 9 mile round trip to a town called Paradise behind a coal-burning steam locomotive in a coach with oil-burning lamps and the good old stove that used to be fired to keep the passengers warm. The famous observation car you may have seen in the movie *Hello, Dolly!* The schedule is followed rain or shine, and in snow time you may see Santa Claus board for a ride too. There is no tax on the fare, and plenty of free parking is available at the station. For a folder write Strasburg Railroad, P.O. Box 96, Strasburg, Pennsylvania 17579 or call (717)687-7522 and off you go!

The Gettysburg Railroad has a choice of long or longer trips (these are through July and August on Friday only at 9:00 a.m.). These too are headed by the "iron horse," as engines were once called, with its whistles and bells and lots of steam. This old road, built in 1873, was first known as the South Mountain Railroad, which ran a route from Carlisle to Hunter's Run to Pine Grove Furnace. The Philadelphia and Reading eventually leased the road in 1891, then merged it into the Reading Company in 1945. For a folder write the Gettysburg Railroad, North Washington Street, P.O. Box 631, Gettysburg, Pennsylvania 17325 or phone (717)334-6932. Tickets are reasonably priced.

While in this vicinity, not to be missed is the Railroad Museum of Pennsylvania just east of Strasburg on State Highway 741 in Lancaster

County. Here you can browse an entire day if part of your heart belongs to railroads, for the story of inventions and developments in railroading is told in this museum. One of the most impressive sights is the enormous mural photograph of the famous Rockville Bridge across the Susquehanna River. There is also a good slide show of railroad history from the past to the present. Do not miss the catwalk! It is a marvelous panorama of all the great engines, passenger cars, and service cars spread out below you: the great Baldwin Locomotive, a wood burner from a Virginia line, a gentleman's business car, and the 2-8-0 locomotives. All were giants of the age of steam. On the way home or before you go, if you are a steam train buff, stop in at the Thomas Newcomen Museum beyond Malvern, Pennsylvania (see text for information and routing). One without the other would never have come into being! For a folder on the Railroad Museum write Box 15, Strasburg, Pennsylvania 17579. For phone information call (717)687-8628. The museum is open Monday through Saturday from 10:00 a.m. to 5:00 p.m. and on Sunday from 11:00 a.m. to 5:00 p.m. It is closed certain holidays. There is a small admission charge.

In the Strasburg area again is a very good Toy Train Museum, which will recall your happy hours on your knees running your own line at Christmastime. This has a wealth of examples from many manufacturers dating from the 1800s to today. There are hundreds on display and three large operating layouts. You can see a good movie too. The whole thing is a trip into nostalgia land for adults and perhaps amazement for the children who have never seen anything but plastic models carrying advertising! The building itself is an old station, which is great. For a flier write P.O. Box 248, Strasburg, Pennsylvania 17579 or call (717)687-8976. This exhibit is a brainchild of the Train Collectors Association, which was founded in 1954 in Yardley, a town near Philadelphia. They have lots of publications, have set a standard of collecting, and at Christmastime they put on one of the best exhibits of "moving trains" in the East. You can learn more or join this association by writing to their business office, Box 248, Strasburg, Pennsylvania 17579.

There are many model train clubs that have annual exhibits, usually at Christmastime. In Gloucester, New Jersey, call (609)456-4719 for their schedules. In Lansdale, Pennsylvania, one group has more than 1,500 feet of track and 240 switches they operate in a landscaped exhibit ((215)362-8890). If you are in the area at holiday time, check the local calendar section of *The Philadelphia Inquirer* for special exhibits. Most of them are operated by the collectors themselves, who will enjoy talking with you when they are "off duty."

The Choo-Choo Barn in Old Strasburg is owned and operated by a model train fan who has pressed his entire family into helping with this layout, which is a diorama of Lancaster County. He has waterfalls, an animated three-ring circus, and even a house on fire to which a tiny fire department responds with great vigor. When the lights dim it becomes night and the house and streets are lighted like a real town. This creates quite an effect! To get to Traintown, U.S.A., take Route 741 at Strasburg, Pennsylvania, or write for their folder at that address. For more information call ((717)687-7911 or (215)593-2108).

You can also ride the "real train" from Philadelphia to Harrisburg, a trip around two hours one way. Go to the 30th Street Station in the city and get a timetable. If it is a shorter excursion you want, go to the Penn Center Station at 16th Street and pick up timetables for Chestnut Hill, the Paoli Local, or the Media lines. They will give you rides lasting about forty minutes one way, and, if your children have never been on a train or if you remember them well, it is great fun. The Paoli Local has some amusing conductors as a plus. This takes you through the Main Line to "the end of the line" and back. If you use one of the Chestnut Hill lines, you can get off at the end, browse through the area, and reboard again to return to Center City (see texts).

For railway fans, there is more than you can do in this area, and there isn't any better way to spend a day or two. It is man's fascination with mechanical power and the never dying thrill of seeing these iron beasts respond to human direction. Good bookstores have entire departments of train lore both local and foreign. And, if you are lucky or peruse local papers in any of the five states of the area, you may pick up a real live auction of genuine railroad memorabilia.

"Board!"

Notes

Renault Winery

Outside of Egg Harbor City, New Jersey, is the winding road that leads to the Renault Winery. A great cask is the landmark at the entrance to the vineyards that were the dream come true of Louis Nicholas Renault more than one hundred years ago. To escape a vineyard plague in Europe, he so successfully transplanted vines here that by 1870 New Jersey was sipping fine champagne that consistently won prizes for excellence. Renault soon became the largest distributor of champagne in the United States.

Prohibition became the law of the land in 1919 but the D'Agostino family, new owners of the company after the death of Renault, were awarded a special government permit to sell Renault Wine Tonic (alcohol 22 percent) as basic medicinal stock in every pharmacy. Following the repeal, D'Agostino bought the California Montebello Winery and the St. George Winery in Fresno and shipped their good product east for blending and bottling.

D'Agostino was killed in a car crash in 1948, leaving the winery and its skills to his sister Maria, who imaginatively added a chateau-style Hospitality House, paved courtyards, and a splashing fountain with myriads of plants. Shade and willow trees line the stream, crossed by a wooden bridge where you will be welcomed by noisy swans and ducks. Inside, the house is like a palazzo of another age with its rich, dark colors and stone walls. Tours scheduled during the day from 10:00 a.m. to 5:00 p.m. weekdays and on Sunday from 1:00 to 5:00 p.m. guide you throughout the stone arcades and huge rooms filled with enormous vats and fruity fragrances. You will enjoy an on-the-spot wine tasting before you enter their shop to make a selection.

There are a restaurant and good picnicking on the grounds. Since they schedule many large, popular wine events, it is wise to call first ((609)965-2111). Admission is charged.

Routing: Go south on Broad Street to Route 76. Go east on Route 76 and cross the Walt Whitman Bridge. Follow signs to the Atlantic City Expressway and take the expressway toward Atlantic City. Exit at Route 17. Take Route 17 east to Route 50 and go north to U.S. 30. Take U.S. 30 east to Bremen Avenue. Turn left onto Bremen Avenue and follow to the winery.

Notes

A Ride on the New Hope Canal

One hundred years before the Revolution it was William Penn who projected plans for a canal to connect the Schuylkill and Susquehanna Rivers to the western land of the King's Grant. Washington as a young surveyor explored trails and waterways in the Alleghenies, and his designs were later incorporated into plans for the Chesapeake and Ohio Canal.

Waterways were once the major traffic routes for the East Coast had only the Atlantic Ocean to link north with south for passengers and cargo, and it was 1810 before work began on the Big Ditch, the Erie Canal.

In 1815 Pennsylvania chartered the Schuylkill Navigation Company to build a canal from the Delaware River to Norristown. It was soon filled with barges, rafts, "arks," and longboats traveling from the coal regions to the port of Philadelphia. To connect with the port of New York, the Delaware and Raritan Canal was established with a junction at Trenton, New Jersey, where the tidewater reached its limit.

Initially, transport vehicles were rafts strapped together. These eventually developed into "arks" with roofs and stable benches for passengers, who paid a set ticket fee. Docks developed, and dockmasters became important persons in the community.

River towns bulged with the advent of steamboats, which soon became floating palaces with luxurious cabins, salons, food, and entertainment. Times for transportation were good!

Drive to New Hope, Bucks County, Pennsylvania, perhaps with stops for antiquing on the way, and enjoy this busy, small town. Stop at the Historical Society in the center of town for canal boat ride schedules and other information. Rides can be two hours long through old cornfields, meadows, stone houses, and old tenant houses. Barges are pulled slowly by mules through this pastoral countryside, and peo-

241

ple on shore will wave at your happy face. There are eateries, small attractive old houses, the old Ferry Tavern of 1727, and lots of shops in which to browse. This town is half Colonial and half Victorian with an ambience all its own.

After New Hope, you might drive to nearby Roosevelt State Park along the old River Road. There you can still see the towpath and the lock machinery used to operate the water flow. It is set in lovely scenery, and you can well imagine the arrival of an Indian canoe on the water.

You are not far from Green Hills Farm or the Mercer Mile to make a good combination day (see text).

Routing: Go north on I-95 to Route 32. Follow Route 32 north to New Hope.

Notes

STARGAZING

S. L. DeCurtis

Stargazing

Stars have always captured the mind of man. For centuries we have longed to know the moon and the starry skies that light us at night. If you have ever looked through a large telescope at the rings of Saturn, you will never forget that strange thrill! The first man on the moon was, of course, the grandest step of all, and we have received a wealth of knowledge and assistance from our satellites and space flights.

The Philadelphia area has many observatories and planetariums some of which offer scheduled shows. Here you can see for yourself with a knowledgeable person to answer questions and point out important sightings. At the New Jersey State Museum in Trenton, there are regular planetarium shows with no admission but required seating tickets picked up thirty minutes before each performance. On clear spring nights after its group meets at 8:00 p.m. they drive to the observatory in Washington Crossing State Park to use its two telescopes. They also have planned courses for a fee.

Universities and colleges around Philadelphia open their observatories to visitors at stated times. Call first, for there may be something special coming up! Some academic centers give astronomy courses, including computers. (The stars may be ages old, but can we spend that much time in their study?) Villanova University on the Main Line (by car or with its own train stop on the Paoli Local) and Haverford College (also a train stop but a distance from the station) accommodate visitors. Swarthmore College in nearby Media has open house once a month. On the Princeton University campus in Princeton, New Jersey, there are special sightings from Peyton Hall on campus. The University of Delaware in Greenville, Delaware, has observation sessions on Monday night during the academic year. Also every other Monday night during July and August you may see stars through their

24-inch telescope. They can only accommodate fifty at a session so call first.

There are many astronomical societies in all three states that welcome beginners or professionals. These societies are glad to meet visitors and swap information and some encourage participation in their research projects. There also is a course in telescope-mirror grinding, meteor shower observations, and seasonal sky watches with much instruction. Classes, times, subjects, and sites may change, so call first for information and possible admissions. The Schuylkill Valley Nature Center, Hagy's Mill Road, Philadelphia, has programs. Call for times and directions. Each clear Friday night the Delaware Astronomical Society meets at the Mt. Cuba Observatory. For up-to-date information call first.

There is something for all stargazers whatever your age or expertise. You may make a new discovery in the study of the stars!

For information call the following numbers: Villanova University, Villanova, Pennsylvania ((215)645-4820); Mendell Hall, Haverford College, Haverford, Pennsylvania ((215)896-1145); Swarthmore College, Swarthmore, Pennsylvania ((215)447-4005); New Jersey State Museum at Washingtons Crossing, New Jersey ((609)292-6333); Princeton University, Princeton, New Jersey ((609)452-3804); Willingboro, New Jersey ((609)346-5000, ext. 403); Mt. Cuba Observatory, Delaware ((302)654-0681 or (215)358-4794).

Routing: Obtain direct routings from each site when you call.

Notes

Steamtown, U.S.A.

Steamtown, U.S.A. is here! No longer assembled in New England, this superb collection of refurbished steam and diesel engines has been brought to a fitting home in Scranton, Pennsylvania.

This city was first known for its agricultural wares throughout the Lehigh Valley, but it soon became evident that it sat atop the largest anthracite deposit in the world. Coal mines stretched for miles underground as this "black diamond" wealth was surfaced to be sent worldwide for fuel. Soon the iron ore of the region was also processed in the rolling mills, and thousands of miles of tracks were being exported for the shining new train lines.

Riding the train was the way to go after the Civil War and into the Twenties. Long freight lines snaked their way to Buffalo and the Great Lakes or east to the terminal at Hoboken, New Jersey, for shipment overseas. Passengers were assured of the latest in clean comfort when they rode the Line of the Phoebe Snow!

But times change. Newer fuels replaced coal, and highways and air travel became more attractive. Time sped on, and the wonderful network of rails was left behind.

Today the grand pillared Lackawanna Station is once again a busy place with a face cleaning and a little, careful restoration. Hotel rooms have taken over the former railroad offices, but the old waiting room remains under its barrel-domed ceiling of Tiffany glass. Brass lights are shining, the mahogany ticket counters gleam, and the doors of the bank vault have swung wide to accommodate telephones. Beautiful imported marble floors are intact, and the unusual mural panels of local scenes wind around the top of the walls in the same bright colors.

Train rides in refurbished passenger cars behind a behemoth of steam are regularly scheduled for a moderate fee and will take you past the city, through woodlands, by a stream, past a lake, a small historic village, and into the Pocono Mountains before you return to inspect the other engines in the yards.

Two excellent restaurants can please every taste, one under the roof of the old boarding platform right by the tracks. Decorated with old signs, walls newspapered with copies of *The Scranton Times,* a miniature railroad that runs round and round under funny black-and-white movies, this place has a charm for all ages.

Bells clang, whistles blow, and the steam is up when "All Aboard" rings out. Then your tickets will be collected by the last remaining conductor of the old Phoebe Snow.

Routing: Take the Schuylkill Expressway west to the Pennsylvania Turnpike. Take the Pennsylvania Turnpike east to the Northeast Extension and go north. Follow signs to Scranton. The Lackawanna Station is at the edge of town and is plainly marked.

Notes

Thomas Newcomen Library and Museum

In quiet Exton, beyond the Main Line of Pennsylvania, you will find a quadrangle of houses in a charming wooded setting much like an English village. Here is a library and museum devoted to the life and discoveries of the great Thomas Newcomen, the Devonshire man of England who harnessed steam to usher in the Industrial Revolution. Born in 1663 into a heritage of ironmongers and shipowners, young Thomas was given an excellent education and encouraged to pursue his inventive schemes.

The ability to produce steam was known in the years before Christ, but it was in 1712 that Newcomen's constant study demonstrated an engine powered by steam that could repeat its motions a definite or indefinite number of times. With the exception of the clock, the world had never witnessed such constant automatic motion!

England's diminished lumber supply to fire furnaces required new sources of power, but the shift to coal presented problems of seepage and flooding of the deep mines. Newcomen's steam engine was the answer and the "timton Old Engine" functioned for sixty years as the only reliable method to drain the mines.

There are more than 2,700 volumes of biography, history, and science in the Newcomen Library, which welcomes visitors year round in its attractive living room like settings with fireplaces, shining pewter, and comfortable armchairs. Additionally, there are more than fifty working models crafted in perfect scale, which a guide can explain to you. In an adjoining building, originally constructed as a chapel, are other fine models that will give you a comprehensive history of the power and uses of steam.

Whether you are an engineer, a model maker, an interested student, or a casual visitor, you will be fascinated. Call (215)363-6600 for hours.

Routing: Take the Schuylkill Expressway west to Route 202. Go south on Route 202 and exit at Route 30. Go west on Route 30 to Ship Road and turn right (Ship Inn on the corner) and follow to Newcomen Road. Thomas Newcomen Library and Museum is on the right.

Notes

Tubing

An early journalist wrote back to England, "Here is a clear stream the color of brandy wine that flows through a beneficent part of the country well set with trees, a road of sorts, abounding in small game and Indians of such a temperate nature that they please themselves in great part with roaming about in a manner mild enough to invite friendship." Thus was the Brandywine River named. It nurtured a fertile valley, provided power for early gristmills, and was a convenient waterway for shallow craft.

The valley was the site of several Revolutionary battles that gave the British a clear road to capture Philadelphia. The battlefields with their headquarters are open to the public. A good film and marked areas for the study of that conflict are provided.

There is also the charming Brandywine Museum at Chadds Ford with always interesting exhibits of Wyeth paintings and special exhibits. Their shop is one of the best.

If it's outdoor water sport you want, try tubing on the Brandywine. Drive down Route 100 past Thompson's Bridge, and you will hear happy tubers of all ages before you see them. Bring your own tube; dress in bathing suit, sneakers, and a cover-up; and use lots of lotion! If you want to rent a tube at a small price, stop at the Fairfax Shopping Center on Concord Pike (Route 202) at the Wilderness Canoe Trips. They will take you to Smith's Point near the Pennsylvania-Delaware line and be ready to pick you up. There is a small charge for tube and transportation. As there are strictly enforced rules against littering of any sort, food and beverages are prohibited.

For a different setting try Shawnee-on-Delaware in the Pennsylvania Poconos (see text). They offer two-hour tube rides as well as riding, golf, waterslides, and picnicking. Reserve tubes in advance by calling (717)223-0770. Rick Praetzel is a very experienced manager and knows the safety rules. He can give you the best directions to get there and will want to know your approximate time of arrival. The Delaware River is about 4 feet deep here, and you will be required to wear life jackets. You will be transported by bus to a take-off spot for a blissful two or three hours. Shawnee also offers a white-water rapids trip for experienced tubers using Foul Rift.

There are parks en route where you can go ashore for people watching now and then or picnicking, which can also be arranged. The Delaware National Recreational Area is on the Pennsylvania border and the Worthington State Forest on the New Jersey side. Float past Tocks Island on a river that has cleansed itself in a natural way. If you are not for a day in or on the water, sit on the veranda of the old Shawnee Hotel, where a century ago elegant guests from Baltimore and Richmond enjoyed a summer holiday.

Point Pleasant Canoe Outfitters, which you may hear about, is having legal difficulties with its neighbors and has often attracted more than 3,000 tubers a day! Better go elsewhere!

Tubing is fun, relaxing, congenial, and economical. The countryside is a pretty one and can be enjoyed from a water view.

Routing: Take the Schuylkill Expressway west to the Pennsylvania Turnpike. Go east on the Pennsylvania Turnpike to the Northeast Extension and take the Northeast Extension to exit U.S. 22. Follow U.S. 22 east to Route 33. Take Route 33 north to Interstate 80 and proceed east to Exit 52. Take Route 202 north (follow the signs) and turn left in about 3 miles at the stop sign to Shawnee Canoe Trips. To phone, call (800)532-8275 if you live in Pennsylvania; out-of-state, call (800)233-8110.

Notes

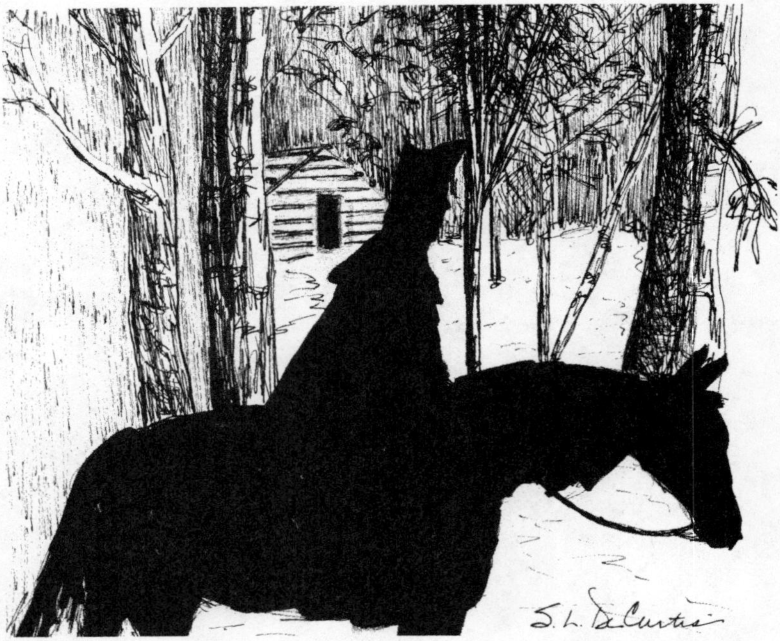
S.L. DeCurtis

Valley Forge

All American history knows the name of General Washington's winter headquarters in his 1777 miserable encampment, Valley Forge. Here his beaten and bedraggled army marched after the devastating defeat by the British at Brandywine (see text).

While General Howe moved to capture Philadelphia, Washington with Lafayette and Wayne shepherded 12,000 weary and wounded into the sheltering Great Valley. Members of the Continental Congress had fled from Philadelphia 15 miles away, taking with them to York the state papers and secretly moving the Liberty Bell into safe hiding.

The choice of Valley Forge was a wise one, for here were fresh water, high ground easily defended, farming countryside for foraging, a generally sympathetic or patriotic populace, and the villages of Ephrata and Yellow Springs to accommodate the growing ranks of ill and wounded. (See text for these sites.)

Blinded by heavy December snowfalls, a frozen Schuylkill River, impassable country roads, no issue for replacement of ragged clothing and shoes, the Continental Army soon suffered the ravages of typhoid, dysentery, and pneumonia. More than 4,000 men were declared unfit for duty, and morale was replaced by disillusion and despondency as Congress ignored the pleas for relief.

The arrival of Friedrich von Steuben, a general of the Prussian Army who was fired by the American cause, soon changed the picture as he reorganized, disciplined, and drilled the fragmented troops into the firm and responsible army that would march victoriously in future battles to the north.

Today Valley Forge National Historical Park is one of our country's national treasures and is kept in fine condition for visitors year round. Special event schedules are full with reenactments, the spectacular hillsides of spring dogwood, open spaces for weekly events, and guided tours.

Begin at the Visitors Center film and exhibition area at the entrance to the park. The artifacts include Washington's sleeping marquee (tent). There is a tape tour for your car taking you through the hundreds of acres: reconstructed huts, the farmhouses used for officers' headquarters, redoubts, the artillery park and parade ground, memorial markers, and the grand Memorial Arch that soars over the grassy slopes. The privately owned Washington Memorial Chapel and Museum in the park are also open to visitors, and during the summer evenings carillon concerts ring throughout the Great Valley.

There are walking and bike trails, a 10-mile bridle trail, a snack bar, historic houses open for visits, and picnicking but no camping. Bicycles may be rented during the summer.

For full information, contact a park ranger or write Valley Forge National Historical Park, Valley Forge, Pennsylvania 19481.

You are only a short distance away from both Freedoms Foundation and the Valley Forge Military Academy and College (see texts).

Routing: Take the Schuylkill Expressway west to Route 202. Go south on Route 202 to the Betzwood Bridge exit. Go west to Route 363 and follow signs to the park entrance.

Notes

Valley Forge Military Academy

This fine boys' school and junior college was founded to provide an orderly, disciplined life and has graduated young men who have assumed leadership roles in all the armed forces as well as in business, law, the arts, and banking.

The campus near Valley Forge is a small, handsome one, and arrangements for tours by appointment are well worth the time ((215)688-3151). You will be turned over to a young cadet after first seeing a short film that explains the many student activities enjoyed by the corps. Six athletic fields, indoor and outdoor pools, a rifle range, an indoor polo pavilion, tennis courts, and a bowling alley are in constant use. The band is much in demand, and their musicians as well as the cadets are proficient in a smart Tattoo and Review. These are open to the public in some months on Sunday.

The Grand Prix Olympic Style Jumping Contest held in early May attracts people from all the states and Canada who fill the stands and enjoy the attractive grounds.

The lovely nondenominational Chapel of St. Cornelius the Centurion is open to the public for services and for sight-seeing. Note particularly the unusual stained glass windows.

Eisenhower Hall houses the Officers Mess and an interesting collection of paintings of former military and naval patriots.

During World War II the school provided basic training for 10,000 Air Cadets and was once the locale for the movie *Taps*.

The cadets are a familiar sight in the town of Wayne in gray military-looking uniforms, particularly when wearing their issue raincoats lined with scarlet.

A visit is well combined with Valley Forge National Historical Park and Freedoms Foundation, both nearby.

Routing: Go west on the Schuylkill Expressway to Route 202. Go south and exit at Warner Road. Take Warner Road which turns into Croton Road. Continue on Croton Road and turn left onto Upper Gulph Road. Turn right at Valley Forge Military Academy.

Notes

Washington Crossing

This is a special spot in Revolutionary history that has been well preserved in attractive, natural surroundings. Here after a grim winter at Valley Forge following the defeat at Brandywine, Washington decided to cross the icebound Delaware to make a surprise attack on the Hessian troops quartered in Trenton, New Jersey.

Commandeering small local craft, including the Durham boats, three divisions assembled to cross near McConkey's Ferry, which was well guarded with cannon. General Lord Stirling was in charge of arrangements and spent a month at Thompson's Mill nearby making his plans. Its large barn stored arms and munitions and meager rations.

The daring plan worked, for the Hessians were busy with Christmas festivities and were overwhelmed by the Colonial troops. Washington scored not only a victory but a most necessary psychological advantage in his pleas with the Continental Congress for more support.

Annually on Christmas Day a reenactment is held with many hundreds of shoreline viewers cheering on the uniformed participants before returning to the Inn Ferry House. It is in a wooded, natural setting, and in the main building there are a short film and a reproduction of the painting we all know.

Bowman's Hill Preserve has a wild-flower garden of great repute, and there are also marked nature trails. Events are scheduled throughout the year, so call ahead for information ((215)493-4076).

You are close to Pennsbury Manor and Historic Fallsington, which make a good combination day.

Routing: Take I-95 north to Route 32. Go north on Route 32 to Washington Crossing.

Waynesborough

The old fieldstone mansion in Paoli that you see standing in beautiful grounds is an expansion of the tiny original structure built in 1715, which consisted of a "keeping room" where cooking and daily living were done and either one or two tiny chambers above for sleeping. The natural fieldstone of which it was built was quarried on the property and was possibly used for other outbuildings as well. In 1724 the property was bought by General Anthony Wayne's grandfather, who quite naturally named it Waynesborough. His son, the general's father, enlarged the house with its roomy center section, and in 1792 it was General Anthony Wayne who added the wing called the "new kitchen." He gave it a wide, welcoming door and the Georgian balance of regular windows of good height, using the curved arches over those in the lower story. Two dormers and a broad chimney finish off the roof, which has a wide eave with dentils.

During the 1700s Waynesborough was a well run plantation and included a large tannery located about half a mile behind the house near a stream. There was a continuous demand for leather, for it was used in saddles and riding equipment, traveling pouches, trunks and bags, vests, trousers, boots, shoes, and ladies' slippers that were worn out of doors. Books and ledgers were bound in rough or tooled leather, and walls of fine domestic libraries were often covered with leather in the English style, dyed in deep shades of ivory, green, cranberry, or russet. Leather was used for upholstery in carriages and sedan chairs used in the city, and frequently in country taverns or hostelries a large piece of tanned leather was thrown over a rough wooden table to accommodate a card game or the counting of money. Frequent travelers and merchants usually carried a smaller piece of leather in which they could wrap valuables fastened with a leather thong or a brass buckle.

The present town of Wayne was included in the 1,000 acres of Waynesborough and were the holdings of various uncles, brothers, and cousins whose properties adjoined the manor house. The Waynes were a popular family and often entertained visitors passing on the Lancaster Pike or those coming to stay by invitation. Among their guests were the notable Franklin; shy, little James Madison, who was to have a larger career; General Henry Knox; and, of course, the vivacious Marquis de Lafayette, on whom one could always count for a lively evening.

Anthony Wayne married Mary Penrose, daughter of a Philadelphia merchant of great success, and with her had two children, Margaretta and Isaac. When the rumblings of the Revolution became more than a disturbance and turned into reality, Anthony Wayne was one of the first to volunteer in the army, where he showed such enterprise and daring in leadership that by 1777 he had achieved the rank of Brigadier General. Never one to be left behind, he fought in every major battle of the Revolution. In the grim winter at Valley Forge after the defeat of Colonial troops at Brandywine, he chose to stay at the encampment with Washington and other selected officers.

At the close of the war, having been wounded three times, he retired to the tranquillity of his home and family, oversaw his farms and cattle, made trips to Philadelphia by horse or carriage, or rode through the beautiful Chester County countryside. He also went to Georgia to investigate a rice plantation that was given to him as compensation for his military service.

Civic duties also called him to serve as a member of the Pennsylvania General Assembly, and in 1787 he must have been delighted to be with his friends as a member of the Convention to ratify the Constitution for which this new country had literally fought, bled, and died. Knowing well that he could count on this intelligent and loyal patriot, Washington again called him into service as a Major General in the post of Commander-in-Chief of the Legions of the United States. This took him deep into the Northwest Territory, where he experienced Indian skirmishes and the Battle of Fallen Timbers. His long journey home was never completed, for he died on December 15, 1796, in the blockhouse of Presque Isle (Erie). A special monument commemorating his valor and long service to his country has been erected at nearby old St. David's Episcopal Church on Valley Forge Road. A visit here would complete the history of this energetic man.

His home, Waynesborough, has been receiving beautiful furnishings, including one or two original pieces from the family, and has been carefully researched and restored. See the good slide presentation first and then take a guided tour through the wide Colonial hall and the lovely dining room with its fine china and chairs. There is also a fascinating room of maps and documents, and upstairs there is a room of memorabilia that bears study. You can still walk into the original tiny house and the large "new kitchen," where you must be sure to inquire about the cradle. You will hardly believe it! The beehive oven will also be explained to you. The grounds are very pleasant as well with a large barn, wonderful old trees, and the famed "boxwood secret hiding place."

This historic house is one of four under the care of the Philadelphia Society for Preservation of Landmarks. There is a small admission for tours, which are given on Tuesday and Thursday from 10:00 a.m. to 4:00 p.m. and on Sunday from 1:00 to 4:00 p.m. (((215)647-1779).

In addition to visiting old St. David's you could go either to Chadds Ford and the Brandywine Battlefield or to nearby Valley Forge National Historical Park.

Routing: Take the Schuylkill Expressway west to Route 202. Go south on Route 202 to the Paoli exit (Route 252). Take Route 252 south, cross over Route 30, and turn right at Waynesborough Road.

Notes

Notes

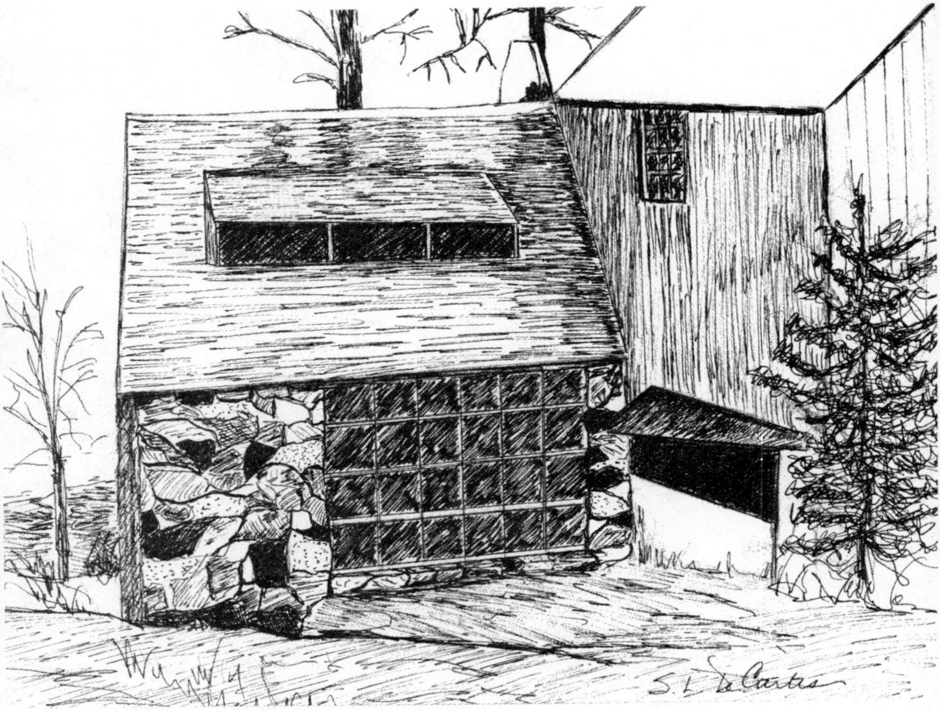

The Wharton Esherick Museum

This is a most unique place, and entering it will be like visiting both the house and studio of a truly creative, original artist. Actually, this is exactly where you are, for the Wharton Esherick Museum is the house and studio of this remarkable craftsman who understood both the beauty and uses of natural woods.

It is set in the hills of the Great Valley near Paoli, where he chose both to live and work because its natural beauty spoke directly to him and his talents. The grounds are entered by a pleasant country road, and your first glimpse of the studio provides a good chance to examine this interesting structure. He spent forty years planning, building, and adding to give full reign to his prolific imagination and skills. Details as well as broad concepts intrigued him, for he carved doors, forged hinges and bolts, shaped gleaming copper sinks, sculpted andirons of wood which he then cast in bronze, and selected and shaped the ceilings, walls, floors, and the fascinating natural wood spiral staircase. Both practicality and humor appear throughout the building.

Born in Philadelphia in 1887, he studied his first interest, painting, at the School of Industrial Art and the prestigious Philadelphia Academy of Fine Arts. Seeking fewer interruptions for his work and recognizing a natural source of supply in the rural area, he moved to suburban Paoli and became engrossed in both painting and carving frames for his works. Subsequently he moved to woodcuts, but it was in sculpture that he found his preferred expression. Gradually he began to design and construct his own furniture, and visitors and friends who came to buy paintings also became enamored with his "conversations with wood" and purchased furnishings as well.

Commissions flowed in for single pieces or entire interiors, and it was not long before his work was included in exhibitions worldwide. Brussels, New York, and Milan showed his various expressions at their

World Fairs. Gallery shows, one-man shows, and then retrospectives followed.

Museum directors and curators realized that Esherick pieces must be included in their permanent holdings as well as in special exhibitions. His work can be found in the Metropolitan Museum in New York, the Library of Congress, the Whitney Museum, the Philadelphia Museum of Art, and, of course, his alma mater, the Pennsylvania Academy of Fine Arts. The Esherick Museum alone contains more than 200 pieces of work representing many media, including paintings, ceramics, woodcuts, prints, his remarkable furniture and utensils that will please both artist and householders, and the house itself, all a product of more than sixty years of creativity.

At his death in 1970, heirs and friends realized that the collection should remain intact and what better place could exist than the house and studio designed and used by the artist? Because of its small size and special hours, admission is by reservation. Tours are one hour in length, and there is a small admission. It is open on Saturday and Sunday only, so write or phone ahead. You will be sent a convenient map with your reservation, or you can take the Paoli Local train to the Paoli stop and take a taxi to the museum. It is closed January and February. For full information and reservations, write The Wharton Esherick Museum, Box 595, Paoli, Pennsylvania 19301 or phone (215)644-5822. Ask for directions.

You are also close to Valley Forge Park, the Pottsgrove Mansion, the Main Line, and sites in the Brandywine Valley. Use your text to combine two or three for a full day's touring.

Notes

Wheatland

There is a magnificent mansion in the Federal style just outside of Lebanon, Pennsylvania, that has been carefully preserved so that you may see yet another period of American history. Wheatland was purchased from a wealthy lawyer by James Buchanan as his home in 1848 when he served as the Secretary of State of this country. "I am now residing in this place," he wrote a friend, "which is an agreeable country residence but a mile and a half away from Lancaster. I hope you may not fail to come this way. I should be delighted with a visit."

And so will you when you see this imposing large brick house with its columned portico entrance. It is well set with four of the original twenty-two acres still intact leaving room for lovely old shade trees. Its rooms saw many distinguished visitors during Buchanan's life there, for here was planned the campaign for his presidency of the United States. The Empire-style dining room is an elegant one, and around its table many important political discussions were held. In its charming Victorian parlor the marriage of his niece, Harriet Lane, was celebrated in a house full of Wheatland's own garden flowers. Buchanan's study, where he spent many important hours, has been kept with his original furnishings, his collection of books, and the familiar objects with which he chose to surround himself.

The large center part of this foursquare house has shuttered windows in the regional style that can be drawn closed for both warmth and safety before being secured with a hand-forged bolt. A band of tall, many-paned windows lights the upper story with a bow window set above the bonneted front doorway. There are two large wings repeating this style with a bow window for each and a series of windows above that. Large dormers cap the roof.

At the end of his presidency Buchanan again sought the country pleasure of his mansion and wrote a book, *Mr. Buchanan's Administra-*

tion on the Eve of the Rebellion. Of course, what followed were the desperate days of our Civil War. In 1868, a few years after the close of the Civil War, Buchanan died here on a June day. Wheatland was the lovely place where he found rest and quiet after his worrisome years in the presidency.

The preservation of this National Historic Landmark has been so careful that original paint can be seen in the interior. Grained woodwork was a popular style in that time and can also be seen along with mantels both in marble and local slate. The rear of the house has been treated well too, with a second portico door looking out over the lawns. There are so many country, Colonial, and Victorian houses around the Philadelphia area that it is a treat to see one of the Federal style so carefully tended and opened to the public.

Tours are given by guides in period dress, and the house is open from April the 1st to November the 30th every day except Thanksgiving. Hours are from 10:00 a.m. to 4:00 p.m. (admission). If you visit on certain days during the Christmas season, you will see a lovely Victorian celebration, but be sure to call first ((717)392-8721).

You are so close to Lancaster itself that you may want to combine visits in this historic area.

Routing: Take the Schuylkill Expressway west to Route 202 and go south on Route 202 to the Route 30 exit. Proceed west on Route 30 to the Downingtown Bypass. Take the bypass and continue west on Route 30 into Lancaster and continue west to Penn Square. After passing through Penn Square, turn onto Route 23 (Marietta Avenue) following signs to Wheatland, 1120 Marietta Avenue.

Notes

T. C. WHEATON & Co.

S. L. DeCurtis

Wheaton Village

Deep in scenic New Jersey and only about forty-five minutes from its shore is the town of Millville, which contains Wheaton Village. In the 1800s during America's growing Industrial Revolution, prospects for the individual artisan grew dim and in some cases disappeared completely. Factory workers or new machines began to replace the single craftsman who had learned and perfected his or her precious skill at an early age, expecting a lifetime of labor. In the past this had been true, and success or acknowledgment easily followed years of devoted work. Here in Wheaton Village you will see the exceptional art of the glassblower or gaffer. As you watch, you will see molten lumps of glass blown into shapes of beauty and endurance in this 1888 glass factory.

You are welcome to stay as long as you like, and ask as many questions as you are able to think of, and you will receive amiable answers to them all. Transformed before your eyes are colored blobs drawn from a roaring furnace to be blown into shimmering glass paperweights enclosing beautiful and intricate patterns, glasses, vases, pitchers, and tiny animals. Only a skilled gaffer knows his furnace, metal rods, and pipes, and in his skillful hands seeing is believing. Bring your camera!

The charming village itself is a quiet reproduction complete with Professor Elias B. Fester's Traveling Medicine Show, the little Centre Grove Schoolhouse, and an 1880 Palermo Train Station with the old wagons and real train within touching distance. Wander about at your own pace, bring a picnic to eat in the grove while young children play on the swings, or help yourself in the cafeteria.

There are shops in the arcade where New Jersey artisans are invited on a rotation basis to demonstrate their skills in tin cutting, pottery, wood carving, weaving, or quilting. The Prince Maurice Pottery is open daily, and you may talk with these people who make nationally known hand-thrown and decorated salt-glazed ware. The heart of the village is, of course, the Museum of Glass with exhibits in four wings around a central court. More than 7,000 beautiful objects are displayed in lighted cases that show the uses of glass from the exquisite to the useful mason jar. As you enter, a copy of the *Victorian Times* newspaper is available to guide you through the attractively furnished rooms echoing the changing tastes of the long Victorian era.

There are also attractive shops on the grounds where you can purchase examples of the works you have seen, as well as a General Store that has old-time candy sticks, many inexpensive items, and a wonderful working nickelodeon! The Arthur Gorham Paperweight Shop has the largest selection of that item in the world, and the Brownstone Emporium has other things to please you. Step into the T. C. Wheaton Pharmacy, a drugstore your grandmother would recognize, and, if the season is right, sample a hand-dipped ice-cream cone in a fruity flavor.

Call the village before you go, for though it is open year round, there are times when it's booked for a large group or there is reconstruction going on. It makes a good and interesting day en route to the Jersey shore or a trip for part of the family while others may want to fish, sail, or swim. It is open except for New Year's Day, Christmas, Easter, and Thanksgiving (phone: (609)825-6800). Admission is charged.

Routing: Go south on Broad Street to Route 76. Take Route 76 east and follow over the Walt Whitman Bridge. Follow signs to the Atlantic City Expressway and take the expressway to Route 47. Go south on Route 47 to Millville and Route 49. Take Route 49 east into Wheaton Village.

Notes

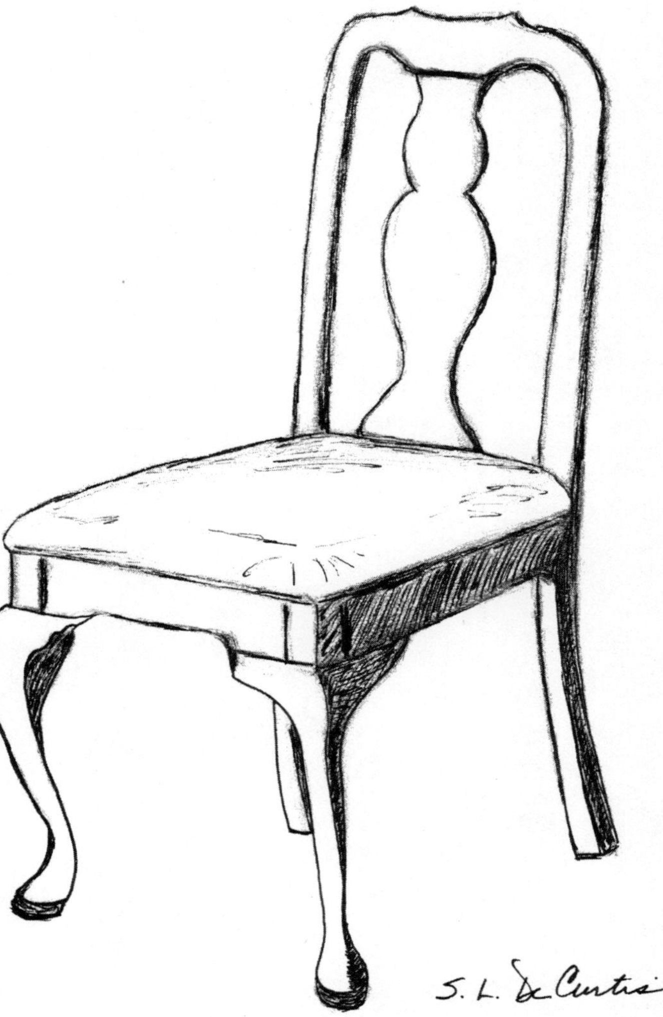
S. L. DeCurtis

Winterthur

There is no other place in the world like the mansion-museum Winterthur with its unbelievable gardens. It is one of the great estates of our country and welcomes visitors from around the world to see and study its incredible collection of furnishings and decorative arts.

It is the culmination of a dream of one man, Henry Francis Du Pont, who with his inherited fortune created 196 fully furnished rooms, each a tribute to a different period of history. More than 50,000 items are in this nine-story building situated on 200 acres. Because of its scope and depth, Winterthur cannot be seen or digested in a short visit. To simplify this, a guided tour of eighteen rooms has proved delightful. (Children under 12 are not admitted, but school groups by reservation are invited to the Touch and Discover Room.) When Henry Du Pont's collection finally outgrew the original residence, he moved to a smaller cottage of thirty rooms and expanded the original house before opening it to the public.

In addition to the superb collection of furnishings and decorative arts, the garden is one of the best in the world, exhibiting naturally placed trees, shrubs, woods, and ponds. At one time this was a completely self-contained 2,200-acre estate near the Brandywine River with sheep, a sawmill, gardens, greenhouses, and prize cattle.

Winterthur also offers a degree program of high repute, remarkable research laboratories, and an extensive library as well as special events such as a Country Fair and the popular point-to-point horse races.

This gift to his country is a rare one donated by Du Pont, who quietly admitted he "did have a good eye." "And," he added, "wealth helps."

Winterthur is open Tuesday through Saturday from 10:00 a.m. to 4:00 p.m. and on major holidays from 12:00 noon to 4:00 p.m. (admission). There is also a garden tram ride available. For reservations and information, phone (302)654-1548.

Routing: Take I-95 south to Wilmington, Delaware. Turn left onto Route 52 and watch for signs to Winterthur.

Notes

Wright's Ferry Mansion

This superbly restored house, which sits on the banks of the Susquehanna River in Pennsylvania, was built in 1738 by an amazing young 28-year-old Quaker lady, who with a small inheritance moved to a virtually uninhabited area beyond Lancaster and York. Astonishing in many ways, Susannah Wright soon spoke the Indian dialects in addition to several European languages. While her brother operated a small ferry across the river, she developed and ran a large, self-contained homestead while corresponding constantly with members of the political parties, Franklin, and others seeking to form the new government. Her industrious nature was once again exhibited when she imported 1,500 silkworms and indeed spun enough silk to send it to Queen Charlotte, King George's wife, to be sewn into a gown for a birthday party. Even General Jeffrey Amherst sported silk stockings of this "Susquehanna fabric"!

She set her interesting house on a rise overlooking the water in one direction and near the main, dusty, rutted trail in the other. Constructed of stone with a wide pent eave overhanging the first story, she had it shingled in an old Germanic style. Doors, woodwork, and the interesting staircase were ordered from Philadelphia. A brick paved entrance floor running the width of the house is another unusual but practical feature. Tall windows were designed to be only three panes wide but eight panes tall and were meant to be curtainless.

Her parlor has been attractively but simply furnished, and the brass fender in front of the fireback sparkles, inviting guests for tea or a sherry flip. In the dining room is a graceful Queen Anne table set with clear blown English goblets. A handsome monteith with its cups seems ready for a posset. The kitchen is furnished for daily use, and upstairs above it is the small room the ferry master occupied with his wife and child. Hannah Wright's own bedroom has a canopied four-poster bed, a small dressing table, and a black bear rug and is paneled with an attractive poplar wood. At the head of the stairs is a small room used as an apothecary, where Susannah mixed the potions every householder must know to care for her own family and neighbors.

The enterprise, energy, interest, and wide circle of international friends Hannah Wright maintained in the wilderness are indeed amazing. Mistress of her own household and way of life, she did not need to be liberated. She was!

Routing: Take the Schuylkill Expressway west and exit onto Route 202 south. Take Route 202 south to Route 30 west and follow to Route 441. Go south on Route 441 to Route 462 west to Columbia, Pennsylvania. Ask local directions to the mansion.

Notes

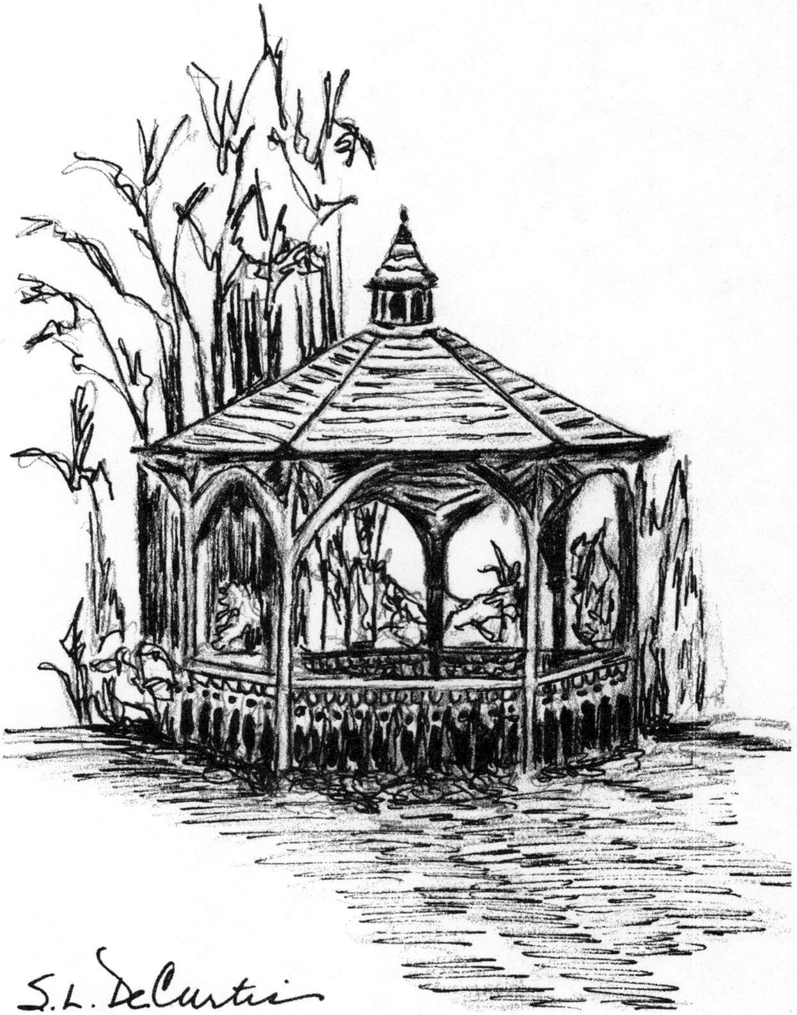
S.L. DeCurtis

Yellow Springs

This country retreat is another historic site of three centuries. Beyond the ridge of the Great Valley and Valley Forge, its lifetime includes a medicinal spot for Lenape Indians, a hospital for Washington's Continental Army, a fashionable spa, an orphans home, a summer art school, and today a "think tank" for experimental cooperation between arts and letters.

After the disastrous Battle of Brandywine the tattered Colonial army retreated to Valley Forge while the British entered Philadelphia. The city fathers fled to York, taking the state papers with them, and a desperate winter lay ahead. Army hospitals were established at Yellow Springs and Ephrata (see text) for two years. When the Army moved north, the recovered soldiers either returned to ranks, were discharged, or moved to larger areas. Yellow Springs resumed its seasonal farm life once more.

It next blossomed into a fashionable spa for guests from the Deep South whose households, servants, and three months' supply of baggage sought "cooler, more generous airs." Traveling up the Chesapeake Bay and the Delaware River, they paused to rest before boarding coaches departing from the Water Works (where the Art Museum now stands) or the packet boat to Norristown. From there they boarded the stage to Yellow Springs. People, trunks, and pets rattled over the mountain road to the roomy hotel with its covered porches under large trees. Pretty gardens, gravel paths, and open fields were noisy with birds. Today the ruins of the old hospital can be seen behind the hotel under honeysuckle vines and bushes.

For spa life, clothing was changed four or five times a day. There was medicinal bathing in iron, sulphur, or magnesium springs, and there were salubrious waters to be drunk. Guests had their own silver mugs at their places in the large dining room for pure spring water at meals. Countryside walks, group exercises with Indian clubs, more "waters" to clear the system of the increased circulation, and naps before dinner readied guests for the evening entertainments. Here were the Chinese Twins with amazing gymnastics, clergy speaking of sin and the soul, visiting poets to read aloud, lantern shows, and musical evenings of song.

There were an accommodating General Store and a Livery Service for mail and errands. On weekends musicians from Philadelphia played for waltzing, followed by a midnight colation and recovery the following week.

Times changed and with it the life of Yellow Springs. Travel to the West and abroad stole away former guests, and following World War II the hotel housed a good art school for the summers. When that proved too costly, other groups used the roadside buildings, which the Friends of Yellow Springs are slowly restoring for a progression of three centuries of historic architectural styles.

The old Yellow Springs Road winds through woods, past fieldstone farms with roomy barns, grazing cattle, and running streams. The old road is still marked, so keep a sharp eye out for the turn onto it in the now-developing area. It is a charming country site welcoming picnics in its meadows under the trees. Now and then a horseback rider may go by. There are country roads to explore, weekend farm sales and auctions, horse shows, and church suppers. You are not far from Valley Forge Park or Freedoms Foundation. For more information call (215)827-7911.

Routing: Take the Schuylkill Expressway west to Route 202. Go south on Route 202 to Route 401. Take Route 401 north to Yellow Springs Road (Route 13).

Notes

York

In 1740 Penn's Proprietors granted permission to lay out a town in Pennsylvania where the Indian Monocacy Trail crossed Codorus Creek. Named for York, England, and bearing the white rose as its emblem, the town prospered to become the county seat.

When the British marched into Philadelphia during the Revolution, it was to York that the Continental Congress fled, carrying with them the state papers. Here the Articles of Confederation were drafted and also the infamous Conway Cabal was hatched to replace Washington with General Gates, who had led the victorious troops at Saratoga. Lafayette, sent to York to raise a brigade to fight the British in Canada, stopped the cabal with his after-dinner toast to General Washington, and the plan by General Thomas Conway was nipped in the bud.

York has been an important site throughout three centuries. In 1825 the 60-foot iron-clad ship *Codorus* was launched there, and in 1831 the first coal locomotive was built here by Phineas Davis, who revved her speed up to an amazing 30 miles an hour! In 1835 local "aeronauts" instigated the new art of ballooning travel, carrying their passengers over the fields and streams of three counties. The Susquehanna-Tidewater Canal ran for 45 miles from Wrightsville, Pennsylvania, to Havre de Grace, Maryland, carrying thousands of coal-and lumber-carrying barges. In the 1850s and 1860s passenger traffic was heavy, and travelers could purchase a ticket to London, England, from little Wrightsville. During the Civil War, General Gordon, on his way to occupy Philadelphia with Confederate troops, sought to ransack York en route, but after negotiations and a sum of money the town was spared. There followed a riotous celebration, which became the first of the famous county fairs.

The town lies in fertile farming country well cared for by many of its

Mennonite citizens, who sell their produce at several local market houses.

Make your first stop at the Historical Society at 250 Market Street. They can give you a large, comprehensive folder noting not only the local points of interest but information on the Indian Steps Museum, Shoe Farms, and Wheatlands, all reasonably nearby. The town of Lancaster, in the heart of the Amish country, is also a compatible visit. At the Historical Society you can walk through a Street of Shops, see an original Conestoga wagon, a collection of military uniforms and weapons, and obtain directions to The Golden Plough Tavern, the Bobb Log House, the General Gates House, and the Colonial Capitol Building. It's a great area for walking! For more information call (717)848-1587.

Routing: Take the Schuylkill Expressway west to Route 202. Exit Route 202 south and follow the exit marked U.S. 30 west. Take Route 30 west to the Downingtown Bypass. Follow the bypass and continue west on Route 30. Follow signs to York.

Notes

About the Author

Boris and Nancy Sokoloff have been international travellers for business and pleasure for many years. Together they visited, unannounced, the sites included in this book and seek to show other travellers the enormous variety of interests to be found in the five-state area included.

Nancy Sokoloff has been associated with the tour and travel business for many years. She has also been widely published with articles appearing in Seventeen, Woman's Day, Brandywine, Bay Sailor, Shoreman, and Upper Shoreman magazines. She was the first person to create recordings particularly for children while heading the Young Peoples and Educational Departments of Columbia Records. Her other works include newstories, plays for Young Peoples Theater, short stories, poetry and puppet plays. She is presently completing in trilogy an historical novel and a fictionalized scene of the world behind the symphonic orchestra. Here, again, her husband has been an invaluable help having recently retired as manager of The Philadelphia Orchestra for fifteen years. Her most recent book has just appeared in Florida and is devoted to Walking Tours on Gasparilla Island.

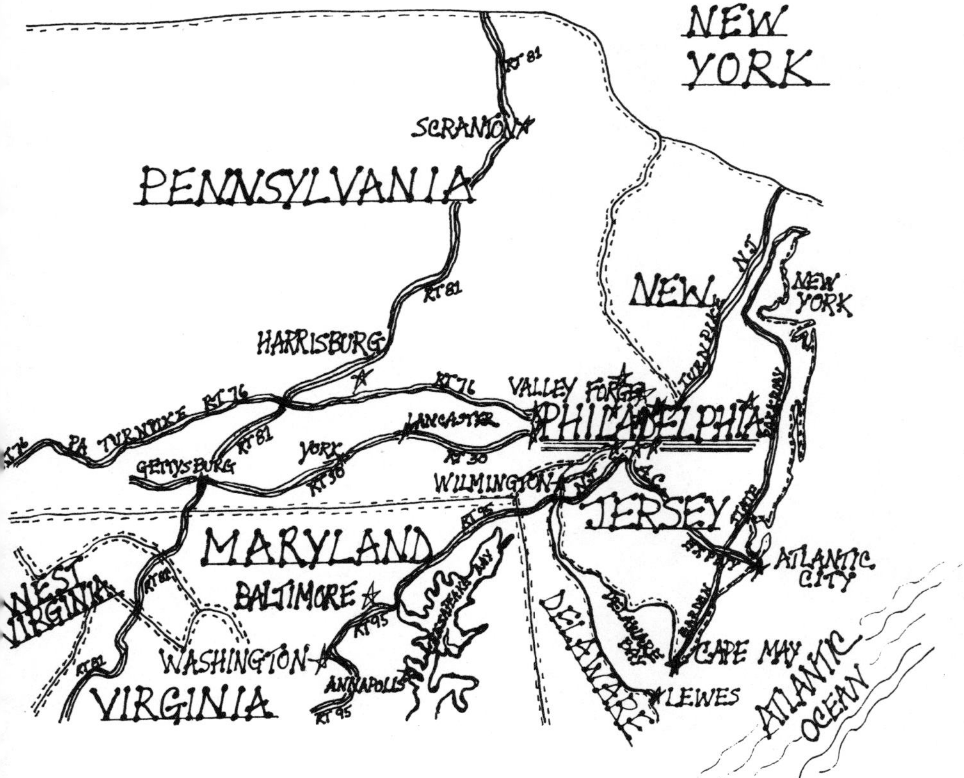
NEW YORK
PENNSYLVANIA
SCRANTON
RT 81
HARRISBURG
RT 76
PA TURNPIKE
VALLEY FORGE
PHILADELPHIA
LANCASTER
YORK
RT 30
GETTYSBURG
WILMINGTON
NEW JERSEY
NEW YORK
N.J. TURNPIKE
A.C.
ATLANTIC CITY
CAPE MAY
LEWES
MARYLAND
BALTIMORE
WASHINGTON
ANNAPOLIS
RT 95
WEST VIRGINIA
VIRGINIA
DELAWARE
ATLANTIC OCEAN

To order 1 or more copies of *PHILADELPHIA PLUS ONE* send 10.95 and the following information to: WHYNOT PRESS, P.O. Box 591 Southeastern, PA 19399-0591.

Name _____

Address _____ ZIP _____

Name on check: (Please print) _____

Send to this address _____

_____ ZIP _____

Payment for $_____ enclosed for (no. of books) _____

(Please add 6% sales tax and $2.00 for handling and delivery. Inquiries may be made by calling: (215) 640-9967)